Business Leaders:
Russell Simmons

Bu$ine$$ Leader$

Russell Simmons

Brian Baughan

MORGAN REYNOLDS

PUBLISHING

Greensboro, North Carolina

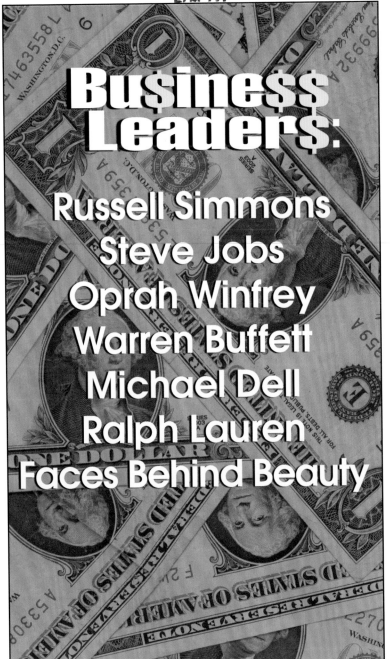

Bu$ine$$ Leader$:

Russell Simmons
Steve Jobs
Oprah Winfrey
Warren Buffett
Michael Dell
Ralph Lauren
Faces Behind Beauty

BUSINESS LEADERS: RUSSELL SIMMONS

Copyright © 2009 by Brian Baughan

Library of Congress Cataloging-in-Publication Data

Baughan, Brian.
  Business leaders : Russell Simmons / by Brian Baughan. -- 1st ed.
    p. cm.
  Includes bibliographical references (p.) and index.
  ISBN-13: 978-1-59935-075-2
  ISBN-10: 1-59935-075-0
  1. Simmons, Russell. 2. Sound recording executives and producers--United
States--Biography. I. Title. II. Title: Russell Simmons.
  ML429.S56B38 2007
  782.421649092--dc22
  [B]

                                      2007037797

Printed in the United States of America
First Edition

Contents

Russell Simmons
(Courtesy of Ron Wolfson/WireImage)

ONE

Street Smart

Years before it became a global industry, the musical genre known as hip-hop was part of an underground cultural movement among African Americans. Hip-hop was born in poor neighborhoods of New York City during the 1970s as a way for urban blacks to express themselves through music, language, fashion, graffiti art, and dancing.

The musical elements of hip-hop evolved at block parties and in small clubs, where local performers developed techniques to keep their audiences entertained. Disc jockeys (DJs) learned how to manipulate records on a turntable in order to extend the instrumental "breaks" in popular songs. During these breaks, dancers (known as b-boys or b-girls) would perform complicated and challenging maneuvers. Sometimes, another performer (an emcee, or MC) would speak or chant rhymes over the beat to amuse the crowd—a talent that became known as rapping.

Simmons grew up in the neighborhood of Jamaica in Queens, New York.

For one young New Yorker, rap music would provide a life-changing experience. Like many young blacks growing up in the New York borough of Queens, Russell Simmons had become involved in gang life and drug dealing. However, his exposure to the early hip-hop sound, with its innovative beats and rhythms, inspired him to give up his criminal activities and turn his attention to promoting hip-hop music instead. Simmons was a visionary—the first person to fully recognize that hip-hop music could appeal to a broad young audience of whites as well as blacks. He also recognized that the appeal of hip-hop culture could expand beyond music, influencing fashion, lifestyles, and language. The exponential growth of hip-hop over the past three decades from an underground fad to a multibillion-dollar industry is due in large part to Russell Simmons's influence.

New York had always been home for Simmons. Born on October 4, 1957, in the central Queens neighborhood of Jamaica, he lived in the borough until he was in his early twenties. During that time his family moved only once, to the nearby working-class neighborhood of Hollis when Russell was eight years old. Life in this part of Queens offered a clear picture of white flight—a trend in which working-class or middle-class white residents move out of racially mixed inner-city areas into newer suburbs. Typically, this shift of population occurs because the residents who are leaving fear increased crime, drug use, and other problems, which they blame on poor black or Hispanic newcomers in their old neighborhoods. "When we moved onto our block there was one white family left," Simmons recalled. "I guess my family was the last straw."

Although the ugly reality of white flight saddened Russell's parents, Evelyn and Daniel Simmons Sr., they were not deterred from fostering pride in their family's African American heritage. Both had graduated from Howard University, a prestigious black college in Washington, D.C. Daniel, who was a high school administrator before becoming a college professor, stressed the importance of a college degree, but as a teacher of black history he also expressed his disdain for elitist blacks who disowned their cultural roots. A politically active man, Daniel advocated for black empowerment and protested against discrimination in housing and employment.

While raising Russell, his older brother Danny, and his younger brother Joey (who was born when Russell was nine), Daniel and Evelyn maintained a strong commitment to their community. Evelyn was a recreation director for the city's department of parks. At night, Daniel ran the community center at the local high school. He was a neighborhood icon, well liked by all—"even by criminals," remembers Danny.

The creative arts were prominent in the Simmons household. Daniel Sr. was well read and wrote poetry, while Evelyn enjoyed painting. With their guidance Russell's brothers found their own artistic passions. Danny aspired to be a painter at an early age, and went on to a career as an artist. Joseph showed an interest in playing drums when he was only ten, and eventually became a member of the groundbreaking rap group Run-D.M.C. Simmons thinks his artistic family, along with his mother's open-mindedness, fostered a special talent in him. "Perhaps I've been good at working with artistic people because, from day one, those are the people I've always known," he said.

Despite Daniel and Evelyn's efforts to channel their children's energies into positive endeavors, as teenagers both Danny and Russell became involved in criminal activities. During the early 1970s the international heroin trade exploded, spreading out from inner-city slums into working-class neighborhoods like Hollis. A stretch along 205th Street, located just a few blocks from the Simmons home, became a major hub for drug trading in Queens. Danny experimented with various drugs, and soon became addicted to heroin. When Daniel and Evelyn finally ran out of practical ways to deal with Danny's addiction, they kicked him out of the house to live with his grandmother. Like Danny, Russell also tried many drugs, particularly marijuana, although he stopped short of doing harder drugs like heroin. To finance his habit, and to ensure a steady stream of pocket money for nice clothing and other things that he craved, Russell also became involved in dealing drugs. Russell soon went from dealing drugs to joining one of New York's many gangs, the Seven Immortals, and in tenth grade he became one of the gang's leaders. While he did not see as much action as might be expected of a gang leader, Russell was involved in one altercation that ended with him shooting at someone. The incident began when a drug dealer nicknamed Red robbed Russell. With the help of a few friends, Russell tracked Red down and cornered him in a backyard. Using a friend's gun, Russell opened fire, though the bullet sailed past Red as he ran from the scene. (Russell would later admit that he regretted this reckless act and that his bad aim that day was a blessing.) Perhaps the only positive outcome of being a member of the Seven Immortals was that he met Paulette "Puppet" Mims, a female member of the gang, whom he dated for several years.

For the next few years Russell continued dealing drugs, spurred on by his natural entrepreneurial drive. By his senior year in high school his father suspected Russell was headed for trouble and tried to keep him occupied with a job at an Orange Julius drink stand in Greenwich Village, a section of Manhattan. However, at a store near the Orange Julius, Russell discovered a legal drug called coca incense, which he realized he could pass off as cocaine to buyers. The scam appealed to Russell because he knew that if the police caught him selling the incense, the penalty would be minimal, because it was not really a narcotic. Russell didn't stop to think about the fact that if a buyer had discovered the goods were not the real thing, he might easily have been killed.

There was nothing about hustling that convinced Russell to make it a long-term endeavor. Still, during his many drug deals he discovered truths he would never forget. Possibly the most important lesson was that the people from the street usually dictated what was cool. "To me the coolest stuff about American culture—be it language, dress or attitude—comes from the underclass," He later commented. "There's an energy and creativity in the ways people from the street move, talk, think, and react to situations I never get tired of."

Russell particularly liked the music that was street—"very ghetto and gritty," as he describes it. For him, the mainstream Motown sound or the bland R&B of the pop charts had nothing on uncompromising R&B groups like the Dells, the Dramatics, and the Moments.

Despite the appeal of street culture, Russell appreciated his native, suburban world for the way it rounded out his experience. Because his parents sent him to an integrated school, he learned the value of interacting with members of different ethnic groups. He had a similar experience in Greenwich Village, a neighborhood historically known for its rich mix of cultures and lifestyles. Rather than observing the differences, Russell noticed the common interests and passions that connected people.

At age eighteen, Russell Simmons enrolled at the City College of New York in 1975; he decided on sociology for a major. His real interests, however, were having fun and networking with the party people at the school. One day, while hanging out in a corner of the student lounge with friends, he met Ruby Toppin, a student who promoted events at a Harlem club called Charles' Gallery. Toppin impressed Simmons because he came from Harlem, the Manhattan neighborhood that Simmons considered the city's mecca of urban culture. He was also excited that Toppin's job meant he could get into the club for free.

The two quickly became friends. Toppin started calling Simmons "Rush," a nickname that stuck with him for good. They agreed that they should start promoting shows as a team, under the name "The Force." On their flyers, which advertised events at Charles' Gallery and another Harlem nightclub, Small's Paradise, the

Simmons in his twenties. (*Courtesy of Waring Abbott/Michael Ochs Archives/Getty Images*)

duo billed themselves as "the force in college parties."

It was in 1977 that Simmons happened upon the new sound called hip-hop. Charles' Gallery usually featured R&B and jazz performers, but one night the club showcased two performers creating a different type of music, which had just begun causing a stir at parties in the Bronx. A disc jockey known as DJ Easy G was playing popular dance records on a pair of turntables, mixing elements of the songs together to create an interesting new sound. Another performer, MC Eddie Cheeba, delivered rapid-fire rhymes over the beat. In this early stage of rap, the DJ and his turntable skills were typically the main attraction, but Simmons was more impressed with Cheeba's performance, particularly the way his rhymes electrified the crowd. The show opened the door to a new world for Simmons, and he walked out of the club determined to become a hip-hop promoter. He and Toppin started frequenting Harlem's nightspots, looking for talented performers and studying the clientele.

The first act they booked was Curtis Walker, a charismatic DJ who got his start at Charles' Gallery. Simmons knew Walker from City College, where he was the program director of the school's radio station. Walker went by the stage name Kool DJ Kurt before Simmons convinced him to perform as Kurtis Blow. When Simmons's company, now named Rush Productions, held its first big party at the Renaissance Ballroom in Queens in late 1977, a decent-sized crowd of mostly City College students turned up to watch Kurtis Blow spin records.

Kurtis Blow *(Courtesy of Michael Ochs Archives/Getty Images)*

A much bigger Rush event followed at Times Square's Hotel Diplomat, attracting more than 2,000 attendees. This time Simmons managed to book Grandmaster Flash, one of the original hip-hop DJs. Until this point Flash had played exclusively at high schools and community centers, but Simmons had promised a big payday at the Hotel Diplomat. He paired Flash with Kurtis Blow, who dominated the show with his magnetic charm and low, booming voice. Flash and Blow soon became a popular combo in other clubs throughout Queens.

While Rush and its new acts continued working the club circuit throughout 1978, Simmons's younger brother was honing his skill on the turntables in the Simmons family's attic in Hollis. Joey Simmons was only thirteen when Kurtis recruited him for his show, dubbing him "DJ Run." They would perform together for a year and a half.

Russell Simmons believed so strongly in being a rap promoter that he did not see the point in continuing his studies at City College. During his senior year in college he told his parents he was going to drop out, a decision that deeply upset his father. Knowing how much Daniel Sr. valued education, Simmons felt guilty about letting him down, but believed too much in hip-hop to let that stand in his way.

Rush Productions had no money, but Simmons did not let this deter him from trying to make Kurtis Blow into hip-hop's first big star. Simmons had a supporter in his mother, she gave her son $2,000 in crisp $100 bills. This money helped him keep Rush Productions afloat while he arranged to get Blow in a studio so he could record a radio single.

The Old School

Like so many forms of music, the foundations of hip-hop are based on the work of a few pioneering artists, whose achievements have been overshadowed by subsequent rap stars. Long before acts managed by Russell Simmons released chart-topping records, three DJs living in the rough neighborhoods of the Bronx had independently developed the new musical form. DJ Kool Herc, Afrika Bambaataa, and Grandmaster Flash gained cult followings at block parties and community centers, dazzling listeners with their turntable skills, which involved rhythmic scratching with vinyl records to accompany dance music and pulling and extending instrumental breaks from funk songs and other recordings.

With the growth of scratching, or turntabling, came the development of other hip-hop expressions defining the "old school:" graffiti art, break dancing, and of course, emceeing. Each of the Bronx DJs performed with their own MCs: Grandmaster Flash was accompanied by a group of talented rappers known as the Furious Five, Kool Herc had Coke La Rock, and Afrika Bambaataa had the Zulu Nation, a hip-hop collective that was composed of DJs, break dancers (b-boys or b-girls), and graffiti artists.

In his book *Hip Hop America*, Nelson George writes that what distinguished the old school from the next generation of artists was the "spirit of openhearted innocence" that favored creative expression over commercial success. With little likelihood of recognition by mainstream record companies, the first hip-hop DJs performed for little or no pay. For them, hip-hop simply was an exciting new art form and a positive alternative to the gang life so prevalent in the Bronx.

TWO

Reproducing the Street Sound

ew people in Simmons's circle celebrated when they first heard The Sugarhill Gang's song "Rapper's Delight" in the fall of 1979. The Sugarhill Gang, the first rap group to hit the radio waves, were unknowns on the New York club circuit, where rising stars like Kurtis Blow and Grandmaster Flash had earned their reputations by thrilling crowds each week. Instead, seasoned producers from Sugar Hill Records, a small company that produced soul and R&B albums, had assembled the group after observing the popularity of rappers at block parties. As far as Simmons and his friends were concerned, The Sugarhill Gang was just a fabrication by a label that had recognized a new fad and wanted to cash in. "Rapper's Delight" was a huge hit, however, becoming the first hip-hop song to appear on the *Billboard* Top 40 pop music chart.

There was something else that vexed Simmons—the grim possibility there would be no rap hit after "Rapper's

In 1979, The Sugarhill Gang became the first rappers to have a Top 40 hit song. *(Courtesy of Michael Ochs Archives/Getty Images)*

Delight." He and a few others had faith in the staying power of hip-hop, but the suits in the record business—the ones who made the important decisions—seemed to view rap music as little more than a novelty. The prospect of the hip-hop movement ending as soon as it had started did not sit well with Simmons, especially when he considered the time he had spent in the studio producing Kurtis Blow's first single, "Christmas Rappin'."

The recording of the song came about through some old-fashioned networking. Simmons had met Robert "Rocky" Ford, a writer for *Billboard* magazine who had been looking to do a story on the new hip-hop scene. The man behind Rush Productions proved to be great material; the articles that Ford penned for *Billboard*, including interviews with Eddie Cheeba and Kurtis Blow, introduced hip-hop to thousands of the magazine's readers. After the stories were published, Simmons hoped Ford would be willing to repay the favor.

Ford was among a handful of acquaintances of Simmons who had inroads with major record labels, so he nagged Ford to help him record Blow.

Ford finally agreed, recruiting J. B. Moore, an advertising salesman for *Billboard*, to help produce the record. After finding jazz musicians and a recording engineer, they booked session time at Greene Street Studios in the SoHo neighborhood of Manhattan. Ford also helped Simmons by convincing Kurtis Blow to take Simmons on as his manager, even though the young promoter had no prior experience managing a performer.

During Blow's recording sessions, Simmons soaked up all he could about music production. Undeterred by his lack of experience, he openly shared his opinions about what Blow was laying down. For him, the song, in which Blow narrates a visit from Santa Claus to a Christmas Eve party, was not gritty enough. It "didn't truly reflect the hard-core b-boy attitude in the street," something that he thought was missing in most hip-hop recordings to that point. But because Ford and Moore were running the sessions, Simmons's criticism was ignored.

After the record was cut, Simmons began to shop "Christmas Rappin'" to record labels. He was determined to convince label representatives that the success of "Rapper's Delight" was not a fluke. After a few failed attempts at courting PolyGram Records, a label he had been sure he could win over, he improvised a way to generate hype for the record. He began playing the song for retailers and telling them to order it from PolyGram. The company's representatives—perplexed by the orders for a nonexistent record, but also intrigued by the sudden demand—took the bait. Mercury Records, a division of PolyGram, agreed to sign Kurtis Blow. Thanks to Simmons's hard work, Blow became the first rapper ever to sign with a major record label.

Simmons first heard "Christmas Rappin'" on a New York radio station on Christmas Eve of 1979. "I ran downstairs. . . . I sat looking at the speakers," Simmons remembers. "A record I made was on the radio. It was an unbelievable moment." The first royalty check he received from "Christmas Rappin'" was large enough for him to move out of his parents' home. He bought a home in Brooklyn and moved in with his girlfriend, Paulette "Puppet" Mims.

Because it was a seasonal record, "Christmas Rappin'" was little more than a novelty. However, enough attention was generated for Kurtis Blow's second single, "The Breaks," to make a serious impact. Released in 1980, "The Breaks" became a top-five smash on the R&B charts, and the first rap record to be certified gold (selling more than 500,000 copies).

As the song scaled the music charts, Simmons received a call inviting Kurtis Blow to embark on a short tour of Europe. Within a day the new star and his manager were crossing the Atlantic, destined for Amsterdam. The attention they received upon their arrival was overwhelming. "I got on a plane, first plane I've ever been on in my life, got off the plane and here are the Dutch guys, the executives, so excited," Simmons remembers. "They said, 'What can we do for you, Mr. Simmons?' And I was like, 'Is my dad here?' . . . That was inspiring to me, to be called Mr. Simmons."

When they returned home, Simmons found it much easier to book shows for Kurtis Blow. Previously, he had only been able to get the rapper jobs in smaller clubs that didn't pay well (and sometimes not at all). However, thanks to the success of "The Breaks," Simmons scored the rapper an opening slot on a national tour with the Commodores, a popular Motown band fronted by singer Lionel Richie. Many concertgoers, unfamiliar with rap, gave Blow a poor welcome when he started his set, but by the end they were out of their seats and dancing, enjoying the new sound.

By this time Simmons had gained significant experience. At twenty-four years old, he had already produced two hit singles, and Rush Management was signing new clients every week. In addition, Simmons also freelanced as a club promoter for PolyGram. The job entailed little more than playing the latest records by PolyGram artists for club DJs, but it served as a great opportunity for Simmons to deepen his contacts in the business. Working a corporate job at PolyGram or elsewhere might have provided him with similar connections, but such a career track did not suit the streetwise promoter. He treasured his experience working outside the building, in the clubs and in the studios.

The success had an impact on his personal life, though, as he found life too hectic to commit to a relationship with Puppet. Leaving the house to her, he moved into an apartment in Queens with Andre Harrell, a friend who was also in the record business. (Harrell would later become president of Uptown Records, a hip-hop and R&B label).

Although his achievements thus far were impressive, Simmons was not yet satisfied. He still had not put the raw street sound he loved on tape. He saw an opportunity when his brother Joey, still performing as DJ Run, began working with a new rapping partner named Darryl "DMC" McDaniels. Run had been bugging Russell to record the duo for some

Run-D.M.C. (from left): DJ Jason "Jam Master Jay" Mizell, Darryl "D.M.C." McDaniels, and Joseph "Run" Simmons *(Courtesy of Frank Micelotta/ImageDirect)*

time. Because they clearly showed potential and had an unmistakably hardcore street style, Simmons decided it was time to put them in the studio. He also offered to be Run and DMC's manager, and from the beginning was closely involved with their development as rappers. He thought the group should simply be called Run-D.M.C., a name that the two rappers accepted with reluctance.

Simmons tapped Larry Smith, who had worked on Kurtis Blow's hits, to coproduce the group's first twelve-inch vinyl single, which would contain two tracks, "It's Like That" and "Sucker MCs." Simmons and Smith were eager to take advantage of the creative freedom they had been denied to that point. The Run-D.M.C. production was totally bare boned—a departure from the polished sound that was dominating black music at the time. The recording that emerged had hardly any melody, just a pounding drumbeat and hard-core rhyming. Simmons himself composed a drumbeat for "Sucker MCs" that other hip-hop artists have copied, and he called coproducing the twelve-inch "the single most creative thing I've ever done."

It was clear to everyone who worked on the record that they were sitting on gold. Simmons felt that even though his other client, Kurtis Blow, was doing well, Mercury Records was not giving his music the marketing support it deserved. He decided to offer Run-D.M.C. to Profile Records, a large independent record label, which he thought might do a better job promoting the group. Profile agreed to sign Run-D.M.C., who by that time had added a third member, DJ Jason "Jam Master Jay" Mizzel.

With record contract in hand, Simmons set out to draw attention to Run-D.M.C. After a failed performance at a Bronx club in spring 1983, during which the audience booed the rappers, Simmons decided to modify the group's image. He thought the checkered sports jackets the rappers had worn to the show misrepresented what they were about. With a goal of making them look as street as possible, the manager and the group developed the iconic Run-D.M.C. look—heavy gold chains, black jackets, fedora hats, and white Adidas sneakers with the laces removed. Rap fans suddenly began to take Run-D.M.C. and their street-tough image more seriously.

Run-D.M.C.'s self-titled debut, released in 1984, was a major hit, becoming the first hip-hop album to sell more than 500,000 copies and receive certification as a gold record. Along with the songs "It's Like That" and "Sucker MCs," the album featured "Rock Box," a track with a

Rick Rubin *(Courtesy of Lisa Haun/ Michael Ochs Archives/Getty Images)*

snarling guitar that married the sounds of hip-hop and rock. Simmons and Larry Smith, who had produced the album, believed that hip-hop and rock were a natural fit because both forms of music shared a sense of rebellion. It was also a marriage that Simmons sensed had vast marketing potential to all record buyers—white fans as well as African Americans and other minorities. With the general MTV audience in mind, Simmons shot a music video for "Rock Box" at Manhattan's Danceteria, a club that had the perfect mix of chic style and street attitude. The video—the first on MTV to feature a rap group—had the mainstream appeal that Simmons had anticipated.

Among the fans who appreciated the combination of rock and hip-hop was a New York University film student named Rick Rubin. Rubin, the only son of wealthy Jewish parents, was obsessed with all types of music: rock, punk, heavy metal, and most recently, hip-hop. After hearing "It's Like That" for the first time, he decided Run-D.M.C. was his new favorite group. Rubin had also begun dabbling as a hip-hop producer. Inspired by the raw sound of Run-D.M.C., he recorded the song "It's Yours" by DJ Jazzy Jay and T. La Rock, one of the first hip-hop tracks to feature a drum machine. Rubin approached the recording intending to capture the mood of a live rap performance, and released "It's Yours" as a twelve-inch single. The sleeve of the record displayed a logo for Def Jam, a fledgling label based in Rubin's dorm room.

The release of "It's Yours" caused a buzz in the underground scene, as b-boys and hip-hop purists heard something they could relate to. Simmons and others at Rush Management also liked the track and wanted to meet its unknown producer. Rubin, meanwhile, was looking to get some advice about how to promote an edgy record like "It's Yours." A friend told him that Russell Simmons was the most successful rap promoter at the moment and that his management company was the biggest in hip-hop.

Simmons and Rubin were finally introduced in the summer of 1984 at a small club that was hosting a premiere party for a hip-hop sketch show called *Graffiti Rock*. The long-haired, bearded Rubin did not fit the image Simmons had of the mastermind behind "It's Yours." "I can't believe you made that record and you're white!" Simmons said in disbelief. "'Cause that's the blackest hip-hop record that's ever been!"

Soon after this first meeting, the two men got together again, this time at Rubin's messy dorm room in Weinstein Hall. Rubin showed Simmons his drum machine and played some beats he had recorded, which in Simmons's opinion were "hit records in the making." In the next few weeks, they began hanging out together—at Rubin's dorm, the Rush

LL Cool J (right) with his band, (from left) Bobcat, E. Love, and Cut Creator *(Courtesy of AP Images/Bob Galbraith)*

office, the studio, dance clubs—all the while sharing their ideas and visions for hip-hop.

They became fast friends, and Rubin did not mind speaking his mind to Simmons. He even criticized his friend's style in clothing, telling Simmons that he did not have to impress record label executives with his suits and that he should dress less "like a substitute teacher." The college student's bluntness and independent attitude had a strong effect on Simmons.

Meanwhile, more and more people heard and were impressed by "It's Yours." In hopes of getting their shot in the recording studio, aspiring rappers began sending demo tapes to the dorm address printed on the record sleeve of the single. One of the tapes that arrived at the dorm was from a sixteen-year-old rapper from Queens calling himself Ladies Love Cool James (his real name was James Todd Smith). Rubin liked what he heard on the demo, and shortly after meeting James, they recorded a track with the help of friend Adam Horovitz

(Ad-Rock of the Beastie Boys). The song "I Need a Beat" followed the blueprint Simmons and Rubin had previously developed with their recordings: a drum machine, vocals, record scratching, and little else. "It's a hit, it's fantastic!" Simmons said when Rubin played it for him.

Both Rubin and Simmons wanted to release the song, but Simmons had grown frustrated doing business with mainstream record labels. He felt they did not understand the music, and only made half-hearted attempts to market the acts he managed. To resolve this problem, Rubin proposed an idea: what if the two of them officially expanded Rubin's Def Jam Records into an independent label and made "I Need a Beat" its first release?

Simmons hesitated at first, as such an independent venture sounded risky. But Rubin would not take no for an answer. "Let's do this together," he insisted. "I'll make all the records, I'll do all the business, and you just be my partner." Impressed by Rubin's confidence, as well as his natural gift for producing great records, Simmons agreed to work with Rubin and establish Def Jam as a proper music label. The pair had little

The Beastie Boys *(Courtesy of Michael Ochs Archives/Getty Images)*

money, however, so Rubin's parents put up $5,000 to cover the start-up costs, while Simmons contributed $1,000.

Def Jam was officially launched in the summer of 1984. Operating out of Rubin's dorm room, the label was staffed by NYU students who, along with Rubin, received college credit for their work. Simmons, meanwhile, divided his time between the Def Jam "office," the recording studio, his Rush office, and being on the road with his artists.

The label soon outgrew the dorm room, thanks in large part to the splash made by teenage sensation Ladies Love Cool James, whose name had been shortened to the enigmatic LL Cool J at Rubin's urging. "I Need a Beat," recorded for only $700, sold more than 100,000 copies. *Radio*, LL's debut full-length album, became Def Jam's first major album release. It was certified gold soon after it hit the shelves in November 1985.

Simmons no longer had to worry about finding clubs to book his clients. Not only were the rappers he managed selling hundreds of thousands of records, he was also closely connected with dozens of venues all over the country and was on a first-name basis with radio DJs and program directors in all the key cities. Fresh Fest, the first all-hip-hop tour Simmons helped promote, was a massive success in the summer of 1984. Featuring Whodini, Run-D.M.C., and Kurtis Blow—all Rush Management acts—the tour stopped in twenty-seven cities and made around $3.5 million; Simmons earned a commission of about $1,200 per night. Clearly, the days of having to go to his parents for loans were over. At just twenty-seven years old, he was described as the "mogul of rap" by the *Wall Street Journal* and had a large stake in a rapidly expanding industry that was growing far beyond the boroughs of New York City.

THREE

Rockin' the Suburbs

Neither Simmons's management company nor his record label fit the mold of a typical company. Food, not cash, served as wages for the label's student staff. The Beastie Boys, who had become Simmons's client and signed with Def Jam, sometimes stormed into the Rush office on their skateboards, carving circles around the desks of employees. Rappers sometimes even slept in the office.

The mayhem of those early days is captured in *Krush Groove*, a movie about a fictional hip-hop label closely based on Def Jam. In the movie a music label owner (based on Russell Simmons and played by Blair Underwood) borrows money from a street hustler in order to press records by Run-D.M.C. (the rappers played themselves). Because the film's plot included many rap performances, it was a great opportunity to promote the Rush and Def Jam rappers. In addition to Run-D.M.C., the film also featured appearances by Kurtis Blow, the Fat Boys, LL Cool J, and the Beastie Boys.

Simmons helped negotiate the deal for the film and was one of the movie's producers. He was eager to market hip-hop to all possible media outlets, and meeting with numerous Hollywood executives helped him establish pivotal industry connections. In his view, the few hip-hop movies that had been made to that point—such as *Rappin'* and *Breakin'*—had missed the mark because they told weak stories and merely exploited rap as a new trend. *Krush Groove* promised to break new ground because it had a compelling script and would feature only the best rappers.

But although Simmons was hopeful about the project, he and Rubin were disappointed with the final cut of *Krush Groove*. Both thought some of the movie's scenes were too sugarcoated and sanitized. Nonetheless, when the film was released in 1985 it earned more than $15 million—more than five times the amount it had cost to make—and introduced a new audience to the Rush and Def Jam rosters. Furthermore, although *Krush Groove* was not a profound artistic statement, it was notable as a major motion picture produced and directed by African Americans, as Hollywood to that point had historically been known for its lack of diversity. "The fact is," Simmons said later, "for any young black male to get a movie made at that time was a major feat."

A few years later, in 1988, Simmons and Rubin produced another picture, *Tougher Than Leather*, which was closer to their original vision for a hip-hop movie. The film was released by Def Pictures, a new studio Simmons helped establish, and starred the members of Run-D.M.C. in a plot to exact revenge on the murderer of a friend. Rubin, who now had a degree in film, served as the director and had a major acting part, and the Beastie Boys and Simmons himself made cameo appearances. For a picture made on a shoestring budget, it was a financial success, taking in $6.2 million at the box office.

During the same period they were making the movies, Simmons and Rubin were also working toward increasing support for their growing stable of Def Jam artists. It was difficult for a small record label to distribute its releases to stores across the nation, so the two entrepreneurs agreed that their best option was to form a partnership with a larger record company in order to solve the distribution challenge. However, both Rubin and Simmons wanted to preserve as much independence for Def Jam as possible, as they did not want to leave their artists at the mercy of a profit-hungry corporation.

Major companies began considering Def Jam in the beginning of 1985, months before the release of the label's first full-length album. One distributor that took a special interest in Def Jam was Columbia Records, the enormous company that represented such music megastars as Bruce Springsteen, Billy Joel, and Michael Jackson. Columbia executives recognized that rap music was starting to catch on in the mainstream, and believed that Def Jam's main acts—LL Cool J and the Beastie Boys—were two of the best and most marketable. They were also impressed that one of Def Jam's co-owners managed Run-D.M.C., still the hottest group in hip-hop. Columbia offered $2 million to Simmons and Rubin, and after a long series of meetings, the deal was sealed in September 1985.

According to the contract between Def Jam and Columbia, Simmons and Rubin would maintain their staff, work in their own office building, and receive financial backing to record their artists and promote them at the street level. In exchange for reaping a decent share of royalties and having final approval of new Def Jam artists, Columbia would take care of national promotion and record distribution. It was one of the largest deals to date between an independent label and a major record company.

Wasting no time, Simmons and Rubin used a large chunk of the $600,000 advance from the Columbia deal to purchase a three-story office building in Greenwich Village. The new space allowed Simmons to consolidate his ventures: Rush Management set up offices on the first floor, while Def Jam took over the second floor. Rubin decided to make the third floor his own apartment, while Simmons, eager to start living in style, moved into a penthouse on ritzy La Guardia Place in Manhattan.

Columbia soon started reaping the profits of their deal with Def Jam, following the emergence of the Beastie Boys. Like Rubin, the Beastie Boys were young Jewish men who had become infatuated with hip-hop. In the months before Def Jam formed, Rubin introduced the three musicians of the group—Adam Yauch (MCA), Mike Diamond (Mike D), and Adam Horovitz (Ad-Rock)—to Simmons. After meeting with the Beastie Boys, Simmons soon began booking them at shows with Kurtis Blow, and then decided to add them to the Rush roster. Not much later, they signed a recording contract with Def Jam.

As with Run-D.M.C., the Beastie Boys had a stage image that Simmons felt needed to be revamped. They had recently done away with their punk style to look more hip-hop, playing shows in red sweat suits with red Pumas. Simmons thought this attempt at authenticity looked forced. "Basically I urged them to be themselves," he says, advice that the Beastie Boys took. Their natural style entailed being coarse pranksters, and also prompted them to mix heavy metal and rock influences into their hip-hop rhyming. Both elements were integral in their first hit, "Fight for Your Right (To Party)." Their bratty style suited Def Jam's own image as the dark horse label, and it also underscored hip-hop's rebellious spirit.

Simmons was aware that some people might not readily accept a white group performing a style of music that was predominantly African American, but as a genuine fan of the Beastie Boys, he believed the music spoke for itself. Nonetheless, many commented on the unusual relationship between a black manager and white rappers. In *Hip Hop America*, Nelson George points out that this "was one of the rare moments in pop history that a successful white group practiced a black music style with a black person so intimately involved in guiding their careers."

Simmons was more forward-thinking than some rap purists about the Beastie Boys. Rather than fretting over any controversy surrounding the group, he believed they were a group that had vast commercial potential and could reach a broader audience than other rappers—specifically, the suburban, predominantly white demographic that had not yet embraced rap. In 1985, when Rush had the chance to book the group for a national tour opening for pop sensation Madonna (whose fans were predominantly white), Simmons seized the moment, waving away Rubin's concerns that the Beasties were not ready to perform for arena-sized audiences. During the tour, their brazen behavior offended many fans, but also won over just as many.

After a long wait the Beastie Boys' debut album, *Licensed to Ill*, was released in 1986. It soon soared to number one on the *Billboard* albums chart. They were the first rap group to take that spot—another first that Simmons and Rubin, the album's producer, could add to their impressive record.

The same year, Simmons helped maintain Run-D.M.C.'s reign over hip-hop by coproducing the group's third and most successful album, *Raising Hell*. With hits like "It's Tricky," "You Be Illin'," and "Walk This Way," *Raising Hell* was yet another landmark for Simmons and company—the first rap album to be certified platinum by selling more than 1 million copies. Rubin produced the group's biggest hit, a collaboration with the rock band Aerosmith on "Walk This Way." It became the first hip-hop track to make *Billboard*'s Top 10 singles charts, and the music video, which featured both groups, was broadcast heavily on MTV.

As Def Jam and Rush Management received a boost from the enormous successes of Run-D.M.C., LL Cool J, and the Beastie Boys, Simmons focused on filling out his staff and identifying the right people to handle the intricate operations of the label and the management firm. Def Jam now had departments handling artists and repertoire (A&R), tour support, publicity, and promotions. Rush also expanded with the important promotion of Lyor Cohen as vice-president. Cohen, who got his start as a tour manager for Run-D.M.C., had proved to be an astute businessman over the previous year. Among the ventures he conceived was Run-D.M.C.'s $5 million endorsement deal with Adidas, capitalizing on the group's love for the company's trademark striped sneakers.

Def Jam may have been a partner with one of the biggest record companies in the world, but it still felt like an independent outfit. The atmosphere in the Rush office was just as dynamic. As Lisa Cortes, an assistant who worked

Simmons stands with Lyor Cohen (right) in 2001. *(Courtesy of Theo Wargo/Wirelmage)*

for Cohen, remembers, "The company always was this great mix. Downtown meets uptown meets socialite meets gangster." Simmons also has fond memories of the workplace, which he called "creative, supportive, and mad open."

Def Jam artists looked out for Rush artists and vice versa. The mutual support between the two companies helped bring new artists to the Def Jam stable. It was Darryl "D.M.C." McDaniels who brought the revolutionary political rap group Public Enemy to Def Jam's attention. After Simmons and Rubin signed the group, they became the label's third act to break into the mainstream with the release of their second album, *It Takes a Nation of Millions to Hold Us Back*, in 1988.

But in the midst of success, there were several underlying issues that created tension at both of Simmons's companies. While the close relations between Rush and Def Jam

Public Enemy *(Courtesy of Michael Ochs Archives/Getty Images)*

offered many cross-marketing opportunities, it was also a source of confusion for nearly everyone involved. Rush and Def Jam shared many of the same bank accounts, and artists as well as employees often wondered which of their three bosses—Simmons, Rubin, or Lyor Cohen—they were supposed to report to. Simmons and Rubin were the primary decision-makers, but they were spending less and less time at the office so that they could produce records, discover new artists, or promote themselves. It was Cohen who stepped in to handle many of the day-to-day concerns of Def Jam's business.

Any label's success relies on a strategy of continually signing new artists, but while looking for the next big star

Simmons and Rubin were neglecting their contracts with rappers who were already signed. Albums by promising acts like Slick Rick, Original Concept, and Nikki D faced major delays, and as a result the artists' careers suffered.

Another major problem was that Simmons and Rubin were letting their individual musical tastes drive their decisions, rather than collaborating on an official Def Jam plan. In 1986 Simmons, drawing on his love for gritty R&B, signed singers Oran "Juice" Jones and Alyson Williams, while Rubin, a longtime fan of heavy metal, signed and recorded thrash outfit Slayer. The diversity in the label's roster was apparent in the soundtrack they released for the movie *Less Than Zero*, which featured old and new Def Jam acts as well as older artists such as Roy Orbison and Aerosmith. However, with the tastes of the Rubin and Simmons becoming so divergent, they were sending out mixed messages about the general direction of the company. Simmons himself was

In 1986, Rick Rubin signed heavy metal band Slayer to Def Jam, a move that caused confusion about the direction of the label. *(Courtesy of Chris Walter/WireImage)*

aware that Def Jam was experiencing "a real cultural and creative separation."

In spite of these issues, Simmons enjoyed his success and the accolades for Rush and Def Jam. Rush remained the biggest management company in rap, owing mostly to the success of Run-D.M.C. During the group's "Raising Hell" tour in 1986, they earned up to $150,000 a night, with Simmons taking home a percentage. Other Rush artists like Whodini, Eric B. & Rakim, and DJ Jazzy Jeff & the Fresh Prince were also exceeding expectations for album and ticket sales. Meanwhile, scores of aspiring rappers were trying to bust through the doors of the Def Jam building, desperate to land an audition with hip-hop's most popular label.

By this point the media was buzzing about the owner of Rush Management and the stake he had claimed in the new industry of hip-hop. A *New York Times* article published in August 1987 reported that at the time six records by Rush artists were listed on *Billboard*'s black album chart. In an interview for the story, Simmons took the opportunity to make bold predictions about hip-hop's future. "Rap will be a fixture the way jazz and rock and roll are," he declared. Not since the 1960s, during the glory days of Motown Records and its founder Berry Gordy, had a music scene dominated by African Americans received so much attention from the mainstream press.

Simmons grew more comfortable with the glamorous life of the record mogul. He regularly hung out at the hippest Manhattan clubs, like Save the Robots, the Milk Bar, and the Palladium. He had frequented these places in the past, but these days he was more business-minded, networking with the movers and shakers of the entertainment world.

His growing status also excused him from the daily grind at the office, and he began conducting much of his business on the phone in his penthouse, sitting on the couch or even lying in bed. If it was necessary to attend a meeting in person, he used the services of his live-in assistant, Mac, to drive him there.

Simmons was keenly aware of how his personal success in a new and hip industry afforded him plenty of dating opportu-

Berry Gordy *(Courtesy of Michael Ochs Archives/Getty Images)*

nities. "To be single, black, and deep into hip-hop was good for attracting women as the culture developed," he noted in his autobiography. He began to have a more selective taste in women, dating models and actresses. He met the first of his new girlfriends, model/actress Shari Headley, on the set of *Krush Groove*, and soon after began dating model/actress Marita Stavrou.

Success was not without its problems and stresses, however. When the Beastie Boys delayed the follow-up to *Licensed to Ill*, Simmons decided to withhold the rappers' royalties until they delivered the second album. Instead of accepting this ultimatum, the group signed a new contract with Capitol Records. Simmons and Rubin felt they should not have to lose the group without compensation, so in December 1988 they filed a $20 million lawsuit against Capitol.

Simmons was torn over the legal battle. He wanted to have his day in court, but it was disheartening for his friendship with the Beastie Boys to end so bitterly. "I hate this, I really hate this situation," Simmons said to a reporter at the time. "I see Mike D. in the street and say, 'Hey, Mike!' and he just runs away because obviously he don't wanna talk to me." (Although they did not speak for more than ten years, Simmons and the Beastie Boys eventually reconciled.)

It was also becoming clear that Simmons and Rubin were not going to find common ground over the direction of their label. They were divided over what was best for Def Jam in their renegotiations with Columbia Records. The original contract had stipulated that Def Jam could secure a better deal if it performed well in its first few years, and with the label enjoying huge record sales in 1987, Simmons and Rubin knew they had gained bargaining power. Rubin wanted Def Jam to reap back-end profits by asking for a larger share of album royalties, while Simmons preferred to sacrifice the royalties so they could acquire more capital for marketing and promotion.

Their growing differences over the artists they wanted to release were equally problematic. Rubin's interest in rock and metal and Simmons's support for R&B artists were not resulting in the album sales that Def Jam needed, and their pet projects were distracting them from the new competition posed by other hip-hop labels. A new sound called New Jack Swing, which combined rap with classic R&B, was catching on and Simmons hoped Def Jam would capitalize on it, but Rubin, an artist before he was a businessman, had no interest in making what he thought was a knee-jerk response to the latest pop trend.

Meanwhile, Simmons's protégé Cohen was gradually shifting Def Jam's focus from making innovative music to selling as many records as possible. Simmons was convinced that Cohen was pursuing the right strategy. "I was a manager and I wanted to break and establish acts," he said. "I knew I couldn't do it on my own. I needed a big company with marketing and promotional muscle like [Columbia] to do that and to *fully* develop the artists' potential." Rubin had no interest in Def Jam's new sales-obsessed business model, and since it was clear that he had neither Simmons's nor Cohen's support, he decided to withdraw from managing the label. He did leave the company on good terms, however, and retained an equal ownership share in Def Jam. Looking to renew his interest in other forms of music besides rap, he moved to Los Angeles to start his own label and focus more on producing records, eventually producing many hit records with a variety of artists such as the Red Hot Chili Peppers, Jay-Z, and Johnny Cash.

Simmons wanted to press on and continue expanding the label. By the summer of 1988 there were twenty-seven artists signed to Rush, and eleven of them were recording for Def Jam. Their success remained the center of Simmons's attention, along with his long-term plans to broaden the commercial market for hip-hop and the culture that it spawned.

The Motown Model

In discussions of popular music, Russell Simmons is often compared to the legendary founder of Motown Records, Berry Gordy. Established in 1959 in Detroit, Gordy's company became the most successful record label of the 1960s. Like Simmons, Gordy is an African American businessman who built up a huge music label on the strength of artists who were predominantly black.

Both of these labels were wildly successful because they won over a racially integrated audience (in other words, they escaped being pigeonholed into an ethnic market that would have been significantly less profitable). According to writer Arthur Kempton, during Motown's heyday white people were buying about 70 percent of the label's records. Def Jam and other rap labels sell to a similar demographic today: the Simmons Lathan Media Group reports that 80 percent of hip-hop consumers are white.

Although Simmons credits the founder of Motown with breaking ground in the entertainment field, he is eager to distinguish his approach from Gordy's, because despite the similarities between the two labels, Def Jam's streetwise sound is dramatically different than the polished soul of Motown. This difference is largely explained by the strategy the two entrepreneurs used to market to the mainstream white audience.

Gordy lived in an era in which racism was more prevalent, so he carefully crafted the clean image of Motown's performers to ensure they would have crossover success with the mainstream white audience. As a result, Motown was known for its wholesome, safe catalogue of music that Gordy called the "Sound of Young America." Gordy was so astute in reaching white listeners that he made it a major priority of the label's Artist Development department. He even hired Maxine Powell, a member of Detroit's black elite, to groom Motown's performers for the stage. Her "charm school" instructed performers on social niceties like the most proper way to shake hands and sit in a chair.

Simmons, on the other hand, refused to cater to anyone's expectations. "I see hip-hop culture as the new American mainstream. We don't change for you; you adapt to us," he wrote in his autobiography. His rebellious spirit mimicked the defiance of punk rock, a music genre that like hip-hop, was an underground movement before it went on to earn millions in record sales.

Unlike Gordy, Simmons rarely gave much thought to the color of his artists' fans. As he writes in *Life and Def,* when he recorded Run-D.M.C. the real priority was not "reaching blacks or whites, but with making new sounds for people who wanted to hear them." Great music, he believed, will attract any fan, black or white.

FOUR

Creating a Hip-Hop Brand

When Columbia settled on a distribution deal with Def Jam in 1985, the corporation considered it an experiment. Columbia and other large companies did not share Simmons's faith that hip-hop would become a fixture of the music market. But in less than three years, Def Jam exceeded everyone's expectations, with two of the label's premier acts, Beastie Boys and LL Cool J, reaching multi-platinum sales. Two other up-and-coming Def Jam acts, Public Enemy and Slick Rick, showed a similar level of commercial potential. By 1988 Simmons, now the sole captain of Def Jam following Rubin's departure, was prepared to negotiate a more lucrative deal with Columbia.

Simmons wanted to establish a joint venture in which Columbia and Def Jam would share the profits from record sales. In exchange for its share of Def Jam's profit, Columbia offered a larger advance, higher royalty rates, and more money to expand the label's staff. The negotiations dragged

Simmons in a recording studio in Queens, New York *(Courtesy of Chi Modu/diverseimages/Getty Images)*

on until 1990, in part because during the late 1980s Sony Corporation purchased Columbia Records.

In the meantime, Def Jam struggled. Two long-awaited albums, LL Cool J's *Walking with a Panther* and Slick Rick's debut, did not meet sales expectations in 1989. Furthermore, while Def Jam tours were usually cash cows, ticket sales were poor for the 1989 Nitro Tour, which featured LL Cool J and Slick Rick as well as rappers from other labels. One reason for the poor performance of the tour was bad publicity stemming from reports that a member of LL Cool J's entourage had been charged with rape.

Simmons felt that Sony's purchase of Columbia was one reason for Def Jam's struggles. He believed Sony executives did not understand that rap was something more than ethnic music, and therefore had failed to properly market Def Jam's artists. "Def Jam does not just make Black music, we make hip music which appeals to a broad audience," Simmons wrote in a 1989 memo to Sony chief Tommy Mottola. This was a stressful time for Simmons, as he faced the possibility that Sony would decide not to renew the distribution deal with Def Jam.

Ultimately, a new deal was worked out between Sony and Def Jam. The arrangement was basically what Simmons had initially proposed: Def Jam would split profits from album sales down the middle with the larger company and would even receive $3 million annually to help offset operating costs. The deal would establish a standard for the way other independent rap labels would secure deals with mainstream record corporations in the future.

Once that issue was resolved, Simmons was ready to tackle new challenges. With Cohen's assistance, the entrepreneur pursued a strategy that he hoped would raise Def Jam's revenue. With a slew of producers and new artists, they decided to create a separate label housing several imprints. The venture, Rush Associated Labels (RAL), included seven separate music labels, including Black Gold, which produced classic R&B; JMJ, run by Run-D.M.C.'s Jam Master Jay; and PRO-division, managed by Public Enemy frontman Chuck D.

It quickly became apparent that RAL would not be successful, however. The records that the imprints released were not marketable, and employees had limited resources to push them. The losses sustained by Rush Associated Labels landed Def Jam in debt. "I was feeling mad pressure," Simmons said later.

Simmons and his employees were also still plagued by confusion regarding the overlap between Rush and Def Jam. With staff of both companies sharing accounts, no one could keep the books straight. Simmons and Cohen finally set themselves to resolving the crisis by forming an umbrella company, Rush Communications, which would oversee the operations of both Rush Management and Def Jam.

Along with settling confusion between the companies, the creation of Rush Communications also initiated Simmons's plan to broaden his reach in the hip-hop market. It was time, he believed, to make the "Def Jam brand seem larger than just that of a record company." Simmons had more on his mind than selling records and managing artists. The recent buzz over a handful of comedy clubs around the country had planted a seed in his mind.

At that time Robin Harris, an African American standup comedian whose act spawned the animated movie *Bebe's Kids*, was performing regularly at the Comedy Act Theater in Los Angeles. His following was predominantly young and African American, and other small clubs that were part of the so-called chitlin circuit also featured acts that catered to young, black audiences. Two things spiked Simmons's curiosity: the attendees were typically hip-hop fans, and the comedians were underexposed. This brand of entertainment, he believed, was the next great place to take Def Jam; the idea for *Russell Simmons' Def Comedy Jam* was born.

Simmons approached a close friend, television production whiz Stan Lathan, about developing a weekly television show featuring the chitlin circuit's best comedians. He then got involved with the management company Brillstein-Grey, which led to the formation of a new venture, Simmons-Lathan-Brillstein-Grey (SLBG) Entertainment, to produce the show and manage the comedians. SLBG pitched a plan to the HBO television network to do four shows featuring a total of sixteen come- dians. Martin Lawrence, a comic who was just making his name in film, was selected as the show's host. HBO gave Simmons the green light, and the show was a hit when it debuted in 1992. The show continued for sev- eral seasons, and a *Def Comedy Jam* national tour was held in 1993, head- lined by Bill Bellamy, who later became an MTV personality.

Comedian Martin Lawrence was picked to host Russell Simmons's Def Comedy Jam when it premiered in 1992. *(Courtesy of AP Images)*

As a result of his successful ventures, Simmons's personal fortune continued to grow, as did his star persona. In 1990 he bought a penthouse triplex formerly owned by singer/actress Cher for $1.6 million. He also entered into a partnership with actor Robert De Niro as co-owner of the Tribeca Bar and Grill. Now more focused on his physical fitness, Simmons began working out in the gym he added to his penthouse's third floor. He also regularly visited a Russian bathhouse that featured a stone sauna, where he would soak up the steam for hours.

Simmons also began sporting a new look, which typically found him in sneakers, chinos, and a polo shirt or argyle sweater. This style was still hip-hop but was a departure from his street image. It was a more appropriate for the new social set he had begun mixing with, the elite who vacationed in St. Barthélemy (also known as St. Barts), a small Caribbean island frequented by the rich, and the Hamptons, a group of glitzy towns on Long Island, New York.

Simmons enjoyed his high-toned vacations, but he also considered them great opportunities for networking. Rush Communications would benefit from having famous contacts, particularly celebrities and Wall Street investors, so Simmons made sure he was on a first-name basis with heavies like record executive Clive Davis, supermodel Naomi Campbell, movie producer Brian Grazer, fashion designer Tommy Hilfiger, and entertainment tycoon Quincy Jones, who became a great mentor. Always the promoter, Simmons also saw how networking could be a free publicity vehicle. "That jet-setting crowd carries messages all over the world," he explained, "and the message that began leaking out from the Hamptons was that hip-hop was fun, accessible music."

Simmons shakes hands with fashion designer Tommy Hilfiger .
(Courtesy of AP Images/Bebeto Matthews)

Rubbing shoulders with the bigwigs also gave Simmons an opportunity to sate his curiosity about potential markets in which to invest.

By this time, his interest in the fashion world had gone beyond chasing six-foot models. By spending more time with people in the business, Simmons was introduced to the elements of the fashion industry, from fabrics and patterns to the buyers and retailers. Tommy Hilfiger was a particularly useful personal resource, because many hip-hop artists had begun to adopt his brand of preppy clothes. Seeing the business through the eyes of one of its most prominent designers, Simmons began to shape new ideas.

What began as a hobby for Simmons turned into a great opportunity to expand his business into a new area. He decided to start his own clothing line called Phat Farm. Introduced in 1992, Phat Farm would not be the first hip-hop fashion

Simmons stands in a showroom for his clothing line, Phat Farm. (Courtesy of AP Images/Shawn Baldwin)

line, but it would distinguish itself from the pack by sporting an image that was, in Simmons's words, "more upscale and aspirational." Espousing a "go with what you know" approach, Simmons envisioned Phat Farm as b-boy formal, fusing the sleekness of hip-hop with the sophistication of the Ivy League.

Simmons needed an experienced partner to handle the retail aspect of the business, so he contacted a friend, SoHo retailer Mark Beguda. The two had initially met when Simmons had shopped at Beguda's store, purchasing expensive dresses for various girlfriends. After deciding to start the company together, Simmons and Beguda opened a Phat Farm store in SoHo. Starting a major clothing company was a risky endeavor, but Simmons's impressive record as an entrepreneur reassured his investors. The rise of Rush Management, which started as a shoestring operation, had led to the creation of the Rush Communications umbrella, while Def Jam, once an upstart indie label, was now a recognizable hip-hop brand. Now that hip-hop had in fact become the new mainstream, millions of American consumers would want to have the records *and* the clothes. But, as Simmons was about to find out, other competitors were about to move in to claim their piece.

Chitlin Circuit

The label given to the string of comedy clubs that spawned *Russell Simmons's Def Comedy Jam*, the new chitlin circuit, refers to a long tradition in entertainment dating back to the nineteenth century. Some of the best stand-up comedians and singers of the twentieth century started in the original chitlin circuit—a national network of nightclubs and theaters that featured African American performers and catered especially to black audiences.

The word *chitlin* is short for chitterlings and refers to pig intestines, a popular meal in African American southern cuisine. In an article published in *GQ* entitled "Notes from the New Chitlin Circuit," writer Devin Friedman explains how the chitlin circuit originated in the age of minstrelsy (1840–1920), a form of comedy in which white entertainers would perform in blackface, imitating African Americans in stereotypical and often derogatory ways. During this era, black entertainers developed their own version of the genre, and gradually modified the acts so that black people were no longer ridiculed.

An advertisement for a minstrel show that depicts white entertainers in blackface. *(Library of Congress)*

Following the civil war and the emancipation of the slaves, white audiences continued to attend minstrel shows, and black minstrels were faced with an uncomfortable decision. They could perform for black audiences for little money, or they could perform for white audiences and reproduce many of the stereotypes of blacks carried over from the original minstrel shows.

Many black entertainers refused to continue the minstrel tradition, which ensured their personal integrity as well as what Friedman calls "the underground economy of black culture." F. A. Barrasso, an Italian immigrant who owned theaters in Memphis, recognized a demand for these black entertainers—comedians as well as musicians and singers—and started Theater Owners Booking Association (TOBA), a circuit of white-owned theaters open to black audiences. Many famous stars performed in TOBA theaters, including Bessie Smith, Count Basie, and Sammy Davis Jr.

The chitlin circuit primarily covered the South and the Midwest. (When he was nineteen years old, comedian Richard Pryor got his start at the Casablanca, a club in Youngstown, Ohio.) Although the Apollo Theater, located in Harlem, did not fall in this region, it was the circuit's most popular venue and over the course of several decades put a host of African American performers on the map, including Ella Fitzgerald, James Brown, Michael Jackson, and Lauryn Hill.

Russell Simmons's Def Comedy Jam capitalized on the growing trend of the new chitlin circuit. The show's first few seasons were wildly popular among African Americans. While some critics took issue with the show's profanity and explicit subject matter, many viewers found the show fresh and daring.

By the third season, however, many people felt the brand of comedy made popular by the show had fallen into disrepute. Friedman believed that the specter of the black minstrel had returned. "*Def Comedy Jam* degenerated into ludicrous profanity and unwatchability," he wrote, "no longer offering jokes, but instead, like minstrelsy, a shrill parody of blackness." Bernie Mac, who appeared on the show before graduating to movies and his own television sitcom, offered his opinion about the new chitlin circuit. "Segregated comedy is sad," he said. "People are missing out. The world's not all black."

FIVE

Feeling the Heat

"**G**ood night. God bless," Simmons would say to the audience at the close of every *Def Comedy Jam* episode. His regular appearances helped promote the program, which he continued to coproduce. Extending Def Jam to the field of comedy proved to be a savvy decision, as the show had a long run on HBO and launched the careers of some of the best comedians in the business, including Bernie Mac, Jamie Foxx, and Cedric the Entertainer.

But some people, unimpressed by the show's commercial success, were critical of its profane language and crude content. Famous African American entertainers like comedian Bill Cosby and actor Sidney Poitier, both of whom were considerably older than Simmons and his audience, and of a different generation, complained that the show poorly represented the black community.

Simmons, who had previously received similar criticism for some of the rap acts he worked with, argued that people only remembered the more profane acts on *Def Comedy Jam*. He believed the crude acts were balanced by straitlaced performers, and also contended that the show's openness to different comedic styles encouraged performers to discuss serious topics. "There was a lot of social and political comedy on the show that gave people insight into important issues," he later explained.

The debate over explicit content—in comedy and rap music—would not lessen over the next few years, in large part on account of a new hip-hop style called gangsta rap, which first caught fire on the West Coast in the late 1980s. In their recordings, acts like Ice-T and N.W.A. bluntly narrated tales about the gangster life that was prevalent in their crime-ridden neighborhoods of Los Angeles. Conservative leaders were up in arms about the new brand of rap that they believed endorsed criminal behavior.

In the same way that he defended the comedians of *Def Comedy Jam*, Simmons stood by the rappers and their freedom of expression. His particular concern was more about competing with these new acts than about their content. Nonetheless, the rap world's gangster elements, both real and dramatized, threw obstacles in the way of Def Jam and other hip-hop labels. One pressing problem was the high insurance costs for booking rap concerts, which had been escalating since 1989 in response to violent incidents that had taken place at numerous hip-hop shows. Stacy Gueraseva, author of *Def Jam, Inc.*, writes that during Public Enemy's national tour in 1990, a Philadelphia venue required the group to take out a policy that cost a startling $35,000, and that some venues refused to host rap concerts.

A more immediate issue facing Simmons and other label owners was that some rappers were actually living the gangster life they liked to dramatize in their songs. During its first five years, Def Jam had skirted a lot of controversy because its artists did not have major criminal records. That changed in 1990 when Slick Rick fired a handgun at his cousin and another man. Both men suffered gunshot wounds but survived, and Rick was charged with attempted murder and placed in an upstate New York prison. Simmons, meanwhile, refused to let Slick Rick's legal troubles prevent him from finishing the follow-up to his debut album. He posted Rick's hefty bond of $800,000, which released the rapper just long enough to record the rest of the album in a nearby hotel.

Simmons also was worried by the poor numbers yielded by Rush Associated Labels (RAL). Originally a solution to bail Def Jam out of debt, RAL failed to be the cash cow that Simmons had hoped it would be. Rather than increasing revenue, the venture was only obscuring the brand-name strength of Def Jam. The company's staff was losing morale as a result, and in the words of one employee, it "really felt like the label had lost its way."

The pressure became severe enough that Simmons started wrestling with insomnia. Danny Simmons remembers that his younger brother was "withdrawn a little bit. You could tell he'd be sort of distant, he wouldn't be connecting fully with stuff." Others were concerned about Simmons. It had become painfully clear that Def Jam had to stop conducting business through RAL. Simmons folded up the imprints and made Cohen, RAL's co-owner, a partner in Def Jam.

The disappointing performance of RAL was at least partially redeemed by the addition of hardcore rap group Onyx, which had been signed by Run-D.M.C. member Jam Master Jay under his imprint. Drawing fans with their shouting delivery and aggressive tracks such as "Slam" and "Throw Ya Gunz," Onyx exploded onto the gangsta rap scene. Simmons also negotiated with an LA-based female rapper, Bo$$, to sign with the new subsidiary Def Jam West. The new imprint was part of Def Jam's strategy of broadening its regional focus to meet the challenge of the new West Coast rappers. With the addition of New Jersey rapper Redman, Def Jam had finished beefing up its roster with enough new acts to pull the label out of its sales slump.

Simmons' new Phat Farm venture carried its share of problems. While the clothing line may not have attracted as much controversy as new gangsta rap or *Def Comedy Jam*, Simmons still labored to get it off the ground. Starting the enterprise required him to invest $500,000 of his own money, and he would continue to throw in more cash in succeeding years. But he remained protective of the brand's image, even if it meant losing revenue in the short run. He refused offers to distribute Phat Farm through what he called ghetto stores that would lead to the company being pigeonholed in the clothing market. "I'm not running an ethnic company," he declared. "I make pink argyle sweaters, for goodness sake." Meanwhile, he took the necessary steps to get the company moving, looking for ways to increase profits and finding advertising opportunities by wearing Phat Farm attire for television appearances and magazine shoots.

Now that he was a fashion magnate, Simmons found even more opportunities to meet models. While attending a fashion show in 1993, he became smitten with a six-foot-tall, half-black, half-Japanese woman strutting the runway.

He was desperate to meet the exotic beauty, and rushed backstage to find her after the show. Her name was Kimora Lee, and after being introduced, Simmons discovered there was much more to Lee than her looks. Although still a teenager she was already a veteran of the modeling industry and sophisticated beyond her years. Lee could speak French, German, Italian, and Japanese, and impressed Simmons with her independence and sense of fun.

Lee's model friends disapproved of Simmons's age—he was more than twice as old as the seventeen-year-old model. Her mother, though, approved of their decision to date not long after they met. Simmons remembers during their early days of dating how easy it had become to impress his St. Barts friends, now that he had a fashion model on his arm who spoke fluent French in all the island's establishments.

Kimora Lee and Simmons
(Courtesy of Ron Galella, Ltd./WireImage)

When their relationship began, Simmons's Rush Communications was doing very well. The company was valued at $34 million, and Simmons had his hand in multiple markets, including management, recording, fashion, and even radio broadcasting. Financial problems persisted, though. Its record sales had dropped off significantly, while its debt with Sony had grown to $20 million, drawing resources away from the company. Sony was considering whether to cut its ties with Def Jam; Simmons and Cohen were also mulling over an exit strategy.

But in 1994 another major record company, PolyGram, offered to buy Def Jam. Ultimately, PolyGram purchased Sony's 50 percent stake in the label for $33 million, relieving Def Jam's debt. Simmons was exhilarated by everything about the new arrangement. PolyGram agreed on a five-year distribution deal, and promised to give the Def Jam executives the freedom to sign and develop new talent.

Simmons believed that maintaining total control over Def Jam was necessary to handle emerging competition from other rap labels. Although Def Jam had pioneered the rap market, its success had opened the field for numerous other players. On the West Coast, a hot sound in gangsta rap known as G-funk (Gangsta-funk) was catching on. The artists who popularized it included rapper/producer Dr. Dre, a former member of N.W.A. and co-founder of the label Death Row Records, as well as his friend Snoop Doggy Dogg. Def Jam's other major competitors were the artists of Bad Boy Records, run by Sean "Puff Daddy" Combs, who like Simmons was a driven entrepreneur from New York. Combs had established his label in 1993, and within a few years Bad Boy stars like Craig Mack and the Notorious B.I.G. were dominating the charts.

Snoop Doggy Dogg helped popularize the West Coast, G-funk style of gangsta rap. *(Courtesy of Al Pereira/Michael Ochs Archives/Getty Images)*

For Def Jam to answer these challenges from rivals, it was crucial that the label's executives identify and sign the country's best new artists before other labels could scoop them up. Artists Montell Jordan and Warren G. were signed shortly after the PolyGram deal was finalized, and soon became two of Def Jam's best-selling acts. Jordan, a native of South Central Los Angeles, complemented Def Jam's roster with his pop-R&B sound and positive attitude. In 1995 he secured platinum status with the party song "This Is How We Do It" and the album of the same name. Nabbing Warren G. was an even greater feat—the rapper was Dr. Dre's brother, and most people expected him to sign with Death Row. Only

Cohen's negotiating savvy and Simmons's star power could have pulled off that deal. A smooth-sounding rapper with an infectious G-Funk style, Warren G. exceeded Simmons's expectations by selling more than 3 million copies of his 1994 debut album, *Regulate . . . G Funk Era.*

In another key addition, Def Jam won a label-bidding war with Bad Boy and Elektra to sign the no-nonsense diva Foxy Brown. Chris Lighty, a producer who worked with several Def Jam acts, believed it was Simmons's marquee status that inspired Brown to finally settle on Def Jam. "When you wanna close . . . and it's full-blown war, that's when you bring Russell out," Lighty said. Platinum sales by Montell Jordan, Warren G., and Foxy Brown—as well as other Def Jam acts—in 1996 helped return the label's sales to a level it had not experienced since 1987.

Although Def Jam was in hot competition for profits with other rap labels during the mid-1990s, Simmons also recognized that he had a unique role to play in the hip-hop community. He was a pioneer of the genre, and because of his success many people looked up to him as an example. Simmons later expressed regret that he had not used his influence to try to prevent the tragic murders of two of hip-hop's biggest stars. Tupac Shakur of Death Row Records was killed in a drive-by shooting in Las Vegas in September 1996. Seven months later, the Notorious B.I.G. (a.k.a. Biggie Smalls) was gunned down in Los Angeles. Shakur and Biggie were not Def Jam artists, but Simmons had personal connections with both rappers. Shakur had acted in a Def Jam Pictures film, *Gridlock'd*, which Simmons had coproduced. As for Biggie, Simmons had been sitting with him during a Soul Train Awards party just ten minutes before the rapper was murdered.

Tupac Shakur was killed in a drive-by shooting in 1996. *(Courtesy of AP Images/Robert Kalfus)*

No arrests were made in connection with either murder (and both remain unsolved today), but many suspected that the murders were a result of a feud between Shakur and Biggie. Simmons placed some of the blame on the media, particularly the hip-hop magazine *Vibe*, for misrepresenting the rappers' rivalry as part of a larger East Coast–West Coast rap war. In Simmons' view, what should have remained nothing more than an internal industry beef was exaggerated as something much more serious, and as a result people outside the circles of Shakur and Biggie were drawn into the conflict. "[N]o one called it the East Coast–West Coast war until *Vibe* named it and, by doing so, inflamed it," he said.

Regardless of who was to blame, the homicides showed how deep some of the fractures were within the hip-hop community, and how out of hand the competitiveness between rappers had become. Simmons realized that as a veteran in the industry, he could have shared his wisdom with younger label heads. "I was 38 at the time. I felt young," he wrote. "But I knew Suge [Knight, CEO of Death Row Records] and I knew [Combs, CEO of Bad Boy], and I should have gotten more in the middle. I regret that. I really do."

Despite the tragedy, Simmons was adamant that gangsta rap itself was not to blame, a view that stood in stark contrast to opponents like activist C. Delores Tucker and U.S. Senator Joseph Lieberman, who in 1995 led a small coalition calling on Time Warner, Death Row's distributor, to stop releasing records with explicit lyrics. Simmons's position was that hip-hop, like any other art form, allowed artists to express themselves and reflect their perception of reality. For many gangsta rappers, that reality entails the harsh ghetto conditions of the communities where they had lived. Simmons felt that no one should censor them, and he was publicly committed to letting rappers express themselves in whatever form that should take. "What [politicians] should be focusing on is changing the conditions that inspire the music they don't like," he said. "If you want better songs, give people better things to write about."

Simmons had already begun trying to give the underprivileged "better things to write about." As a man of wealth and influence he wanted to do something to help end poverty and gang violence, so in 1995 he established the Rush Philanthropic Arts Foundation with his two brothers. This nonprofit organization, which remains active today, is dedicated to providing disadvantaged youth with opportunities to become involved in the arts. Danny Simmons, now a recognized painter, has been able to use his contacts in the art world to establish exhibition spaces for young artists. Russell's most direct contribution to the program has been overseeing the organization's Rush Impact Mentorship Initiative, which brings young people to Phat Farm for a behind-the-scenes look at the business and offers them a chance to learn from the company's staff about working in the fashion industry.

Co-founding the nonprofit was part of a dramatic change in Simmons. He began eating healthier food; he overcame his insomnia; and he stopped worrying so much about the bottom line, or about things he couldn't control. These changes, he claimed, all resulted from discovering a centuries-old spiritual tradition that gave him a peace he had not known before: yoga.

SIX

A Quieted Mind

For someone born and raised in gray, cold New York, sunny Los Angeles was a completely different world. During the mid-1990s, Simmons's taste for glamour and his desire to network with the Hollywood elite regularly brought him to the West Coast. But he found more than movie deals and fancy parties. In a studio in the posh neighborhood of Brentwood, he was introduced to yoga, an ancient form of meditation that influenced changes in his business practices, ethics, and the way he viewed the world.

As a city that closely followed the hippest trends in wellness and spirituality, Los Angeles had a large number of yoga students. One of these was Bobby Shriver, a producer friend of Simmons who invited him along to one of his classes. When Simmons entered the studio, he was first pleased to find that the women of the class, mostly models and actresses, far outnumbered the men. He also immediately warmed to

Simmons found that practicing yoga calmed his mind and provided inner peace. *(Courtesy of George Pimentel/WireImage)*

the instructor, a former monk who played the music of Tupac or R&B during class instead of the New Age music that was more common to yoga sessions.

What most impressed Simmons, however, was the practice itself. When he began meditating in the various yogic postures known as asana, he found he could quiet his mind and feel less anxious about his business concerns. "I got addicted right away," he remembers.

Soon yoga became part of Simmons's daily routine. "Yoga changed my life dramatically," he said. "Before yoga, I was an insomniac. I couldn't sleep. I was worried about a bunch of stuff that I couldn't change. But I started to let go of wasteful ideas. I learned to be at peace." Yoga also inspired Simmons to adopt certain spiritual principles, such as avoiding harm to all sentient beings. As a result he became a vegan, meaning he does not eat meat or any products of animals. His new ethical stance attracted offers to do promotional spots for People for the Ethical Treatment of Animals (PETA) and other animal-rights organizations.

But despite the changes in his demeanor and his diet, Simmons remained ambitious. Nothing would sway him from his commitment to the continual growth of his businesses. But while he remained a driven entrepreneur, with the new benefits of meditation he found that he could approach difficult business decisions with greater composure and focus.

One of his first major moves after he took up the practice of yoga was to close down Rush Management. Simmons had decided that the personal attention that artists required placed too many demands on his time. To keep his management interests going, he became a partner in SLBG Management, manned by the people with whom he had collaborated on *Def Comedy Jam*. At the same time, Simmons established new operations in publishing, advertising, film, and television.

OneWorld magazine, introduced in 1995, aimed to compete with other hip-hop monthlies like *The Source* and *Vibe*. The magazine venture birthed the *One World Music Beat* television show in 1998. The program mixed performance clips with celebrity interviews, and, for a spell, Kimora Lee served as host.

DJ Clue (background left) stands with four popular Def Jam rappers: Redman (foreground left), DMX (background middle), Method Man (second from right), and Jay-Z (far right). *(Courtesy of AP Images/Kathy Willens)*

Rush Media, an advertising company Simmons established in 1996, was much more profitable than the *OneWorld* ventures. Catering to the American youth culture market, Rush Media quickly attracted big-name clients like HBO, Estée Lauder, Tommy Hilfiger, and Coca-Cola.

It was inevitable that an entertainment mogul like Simmons would seek greater involvement in the film market. In 1997 Simmons landed a spot as executive producer for the gritty drama *Gridlock'd,* starring Tupac Shakur and Tim Roth as heroin addicts. The film, a Def Pictures release and one of Shakur's final acting performances, played well with critics and grossed more than $5 million. Another movie that Def Pictures released that year, the comedy *How to Be a Player*, also scored at the box office. Starring Bill Bellamy of *Def Comedy Jam* fame, the film featured a soundtrack with songs by Def Jam stars Foxy Brown, EPMD, and Redman.

One of the biggest challenges of Simmons's career turned out to be making his clothing line a moneymaking operation. Because he had been busy with so many different ventures, Phat Farm suffered, but the situation improved once Simmons began to focus more of his attention on the clothing company. In 1996, after six years in operation and his own investment of $10 million to keep the company afloat, Phat Farm started turning a profit.

In addition to these changes in his professional life, Russell Simmons made a major personal life change when he asked his girlfriend Kimora Lee to marry him. The two had dated for five years. Two ceremonies were held, a small civil ceremony in Manhattan on December 20, 1998, and then a larger service on St. Barts a few days later. Simmons's brother Joey, who had undergone a spiritual conversion of his own and had become a Christian minister, conducted the service. Celebrities attending the island wedding included home-decorating guru Martha Stewart, entertainment magnate Sean "Diddy" Combs, movie producer Penny Marshall, and longtime Simmons friend Andre Harrell.

After the wedding, the couple returned to New York and bought a penthouse loft from guitarist Keith Richards of the Rolling Stones for $2 million, located in the Wall Street district of Manhattan. Simmons, eager to establish a yoga routine at home, installed a meditation room. One of the quirks of the loft was that it had two refrigerators, one filled with Russell's vegan food and the other for his meat-eating wife.

Because of his busy personal and professional life, Simmons had little time to engage in the daily business of Def Jam. With Cohen running the show, however, his presence was not required. "The truth is," Simmons wrote, "the more I got away from Def Jam on a day-to-day basis, the better the company did." Under Cohen's leadership Def Jam finished the 1990s buoyed by the successes of Redman, Method Man, and Foxy Brown, as well as newcomers DMX, Ja Rule, and Jay-Z, a former drug dealer who went on to become "the greatest MC of all time," according to an MTV poll.

In 1998, Simmons and Cohen began to contemplate selling Def Jam. Their arrangement with parent company PolyGram, which by that time owned 60 percent of the company, had not produced the results that the two men had hoped for. Simmons and Cohen, now two of the most respected executives in the record business, were aware that they had plenty of negotiating power. Simmons balked when PolyGram made a bid to buy Def Jam for $50 million. He wanted more money because of the value of artists like DMX and Jay-Z, whose contracts he wanted to include in the deal. Holding out proved to be the best thing Simmons could do, because in November 1998 Seagram's Universal Music Group (UMG), the world's largest record company, bought PolyGram and its stake in Def Jam. Cohen and Simmons ended up selling their shares in Def Jam to UMG for $130 million in 1999, netting Simmons a sizable return on the $1,000 he had invested to start Def Jam back in 1984.

Although Simmons no longer owned Def Jam, he wanted to remain involved with the rap music business and so retained the title of chairman. He balanced his Def Jam affairs with managing his other enterprises. Simmons's advertising company was doing particularly well. After achieving impressive growth over its first few years, in 1999 it forged a profitable partnership with Deutsch, Inc., one of the world's most prominent advertising agencies with annual revenue of $1 billion.

But by this time Simmons's hottest enterprise, surprisingly, was Phat Farm. Simmons may have missed out on short-term revenue by passing up clothing trends, but his careful efforts to develop the brand value of Phat Farm's classic look paid long-term dividends. In 2000, a women's clothing line, Baby Phat, was added, and it soon surpassed the men's line in revenue. Kimora Lee Simmons began running the women's line shortly after it was established, and as creative director she quickly showed a knack for turning profits that matched her husband's. In addition, as "the face of the 21st century" (a title given to her by fashion designer Karl Lagerfeld), she was an ideal spokesmodel for Baby Phat.

Phat Fashions' success inspired two other major hip-hop figures, Sean Combs and Jay-Z, to start their own urban-lifestyle clothing lines in the late 1990s. Combs's Sean John line and Jay-Z's Rocawear would also develop into major corporations. By extending their business interests beyond the music sector, Combs and Jay-Z were following an industry precedent some have called the "Russell Effect"—a perfect illustration that wherever Simmons has gone, the hip-hop community has followed. And as the twenty-first century approached, it was certain that his pioneering spirit would lead hip-hop into more uncharted areas.

SEVEN

Assembling an Army

It was during Simmons's reading of *The Yoga Sutras of Patanjali*, the "bible" of yoga and one of his favorite books, that he discovered a simple truth about living. "[T]he only real happiness is the kind that comes from within," Simmons said, "and I believe that my happiness only comes from serving other people." It was a startling about-face for someone as profit-minded as Simmons—by his own admission, the first forty years of his life "were about consumption and money and power." But clearly, another major change had occurred, and many people shared his hope that the years to come would be dedicated to public service.

By this point, no one was surprised that he aimed to include hip-hop in his new mission. In 2000, he launched a political awareness campaign called Rap the Vote. Its central mission was to boost voting among urban youth, a segment of the population that has been known for its lack of participation in U.S. elections. To appeal to this target group, Simmons booked television and radio spots featuring LL Cool J, P. Diddy (the stage name of Sean Combs), and other rappers and actors.

In Simmons's opinion the hip-hop community had the power to not only get young people to the polls, but also to influence how they thought about important issues. "The hip hop community moves as an army—on issues, on politics, on social condi-

Simmons speaks to reporters during the 2002 Rap the Vote campaign drive. *(Courtesy of AP Images/Ed Bailey)*

tions, on subject matter," he said. "They choose a car, that car is hot. They choose a watch, that watch is hot. . . . And when they choose a potential president, it's the same thing."

With that conviction in mind, Simmons organized the first Hip-Hop Summit, a conference for the hip-hop community and other interested individuals to openly discuss issues such as free speech rights and artistic responsibility. The summit, which was held in June 2001 in New York City, was attended by influential hip-hop figures like LL Cool J, Chuck D, and Suge Knight, along with respected individuals like scholar/ author Michael Eric Dyson and Kweisi Mfume, president of the National Association for the Advancement of Colored People (NAACP). Harvard professor Cornel West spoke at

Simmons speaks to the crowd at the 2004 Boston Hip-Hop Summit.
(Courtesy of AP Images/Lisa Poole)

the event, and Nation of Islam leader Louis Farrakhan delivered the keynote address.

The summit was considered such a success that a month later the Hip-Hop Summit Action Network (HSAN), a political action committee, was formed. Simmons stepped up to be the organization's chairman while Benjamin Chavis Muhammad, a veteran advocate for civil rights, oversaw daily operations as HSAN's president and CEO. After a year of brainstorming, in 2002 HSAN published "What We Want," a fifteen-point document mission statement that included pledges to address discrimination, poverty, HIV/AIDS awareness, education reform, and harsh mandatory sentencing penalties for drug-related offenses.

One legal issue that particularly troubled Simmons and HSAN was government authorities' recent crackdown on rap music with explicit lyrics. In June 2001 the Federal Communications Commission (FCC) imposed a $7,000 fine on a radio station for airing rapper Eminem's song "The Real Slim Shady." The fine came in the wake of the introduction of the Media Marketing Accountability Act (MMAA), a Senate bill intended to prohibit the marketing of music, movies, and video and computer games with explicit content to people under the age of seventeen. The main proponents of the bill were Senators Hillary Rodham Clinton and Joseph Lieberman, a legislator who in previous years had been a thorn in the rap community's side.

HSAN believed the bill was an attack on the recording industry and on artistic expression in general. During a July 2001 hearing Simmons took the chance to present HSAN's opposition to the bill in a written statement addressed to the U.S. Senate Committee on Government Affairs. Since Simmons was not invited to the committee hearings, he asked Hilary Rosen, president and CEO of the Recording Industry Association of America (RIAA), to read the statement in his place.

Simmons's testimonial stressed that the hip-hop community recognized the need to take a critical look at some of rap's lyrics and that HSAN was committed to improving "the artistic presentation of [its] culture and experience." However, Simmons argued that the best kind of change takes place within the industry, through the efforts of HSAN and other organizations, while legislation like the MMAA is the sort of unconstitutional government constraint that denies free speech and obstructs the hip-hop community's commitment to tell the truth about the street.

The protest had a significant impact, as support for the bill never gathered enough momentum to become a law. Rosen praised HSAN for its efforts. "The Hip-Hop Summit

Action Network single-handedly got Senator Lieberman off our backs in regard to his legislation," the RIAA president said.

But HSAN still had not yet passed muster for many people within the hip-hop community. *The Source*, a magazine that some call the bible of hip-hop, was slow to officially endorse HSAN, and in May 2002 the magazine's editors raised concerns that HSAN was more a trade organization than a political action committee, and that it was ignoring larger issues in favor of its anti-censorship drive. Such a focus had as much to do with ensuring album sales as preserving free speech rights. Chuck D, an outspoken activist, held similar doubts about HSAN. "How you gonna be on the industry's payroll and speak out?" he argued.

Simmons was open to the criticism and interested in keeping the dialogue going. For an article co-written with Benjamin Muhammad and published in *The Source* in June 2002, he acknowledged that poverty, homelessness, illiteracy, police brutality, and a host of other issues were more important than preserving the First Amendment rights of musicians and other artists. Simmons and Muhammad explained that, as HSAN had stated in its fifteen-point agenda, the organization was committed to dealing with issues in real ways.

One way HSAN fulfilled its promise was organizing the Hip Hop Reader Program, a literacy campaign that recruited public high-school students to read and discuss books, poetry, and lyrics picked by rappers, authors, and community leaders. The program gave incentives for students to read by awarding prizes for finishing the books on the Hip Hop Reader list. Simmons, of course, could not resist doing a little cross-marketing through the program: *Life and Def,* his autobiography, was included as a reading selection, and Phat Farm apparel was among the prizes.

HSAN's voter drive, however, attracted more media attention and made a bigger impact. Shortly after it was established, HSAN stated its ambitious goal of signing up 2 million new voters for the 2004 presidential election. It was an important mission in light of the low numbers of young people who had turned out to vote in recent election years. According to the Center for Information and Research on Civic Learning and Engagement (CIRCLE), only 16 million people under the age of thirty had voted in the 2000 presidential election. Simmons recognized the connection hip-hop's stars have with many younger citizens—a point of contact that politicians and other public figures lack. The Hip-Hop Summits were the way to capitalize on that connection. "When [P. Diddy] says register to vote, maybe people will do it," Simmons said. "The most important thing we gotta do is make it cool to show up at the rallies, make it in style to pay attention."

Since the first hip-hop summit in 2001, more than forty similar summits have been held in major cities all over the country. Most of the events focused on registering young people to vote, and scored positive results leading up to the 2004 presidential election. Using his clout as a hip-hop mogul, Simmons tapped a number of hip-hop celebrities to host events, including Will Smith, LL Cool J, Eminem, Master P, Snoop Dogg, and Beyoncé. He also recruited the mayors of each of the cities to take part in the proceedings.

Young attendees registered to vote in droves. Simmons announced that the Houston summit in 2004 registered 25,000 voters, while the Philadelphia summit managed to sign up nearly 80,000. Other cities reported similarly high numbers. Owing in part to the summits and other voter-registration drives, in 2004 there was an increase in voting among the target population. CIRCLE reported that nearly 21 million voters under the age of thirty showed up at the polls for the 2004 presidential election; according to CBS News, there were almost 5 million more voters in that age group since the previous presidential election, marking an increase of 22 percent.

Hip-Hop Activism

Russell Simmons helped bring hip-hop activism into the national spotlight through his work with Hi--Hop Summit Action Network, but he was not the first to marry hip-hop and politics. During the mid-1980s, journalist and Public Enemy member Harry Allen coined the term "hip-hop activism" to describe a growing trend among rap artists. By that time hip-hop had become a large enough force to unify rappers such as Melle Mel, Afrika Bambaataa and Soul Sonic Force, and Run-D.M.C. in fighting political causes like ending the nuclear arms race and protesting apartheid in South Africa.

There is a long tradition of political advocacy in the history of black music. One of the best-known black musicians of the 1960s civil rights movement was calypso singer Harry Belafonte, who helped raise funds for the Southern Christian Leadership Conference (SCLC) led by Martin Luther King Jr. In later years, soul singers Curtis Mayfield, Marvin Gaye, and Stevie Wonder addressed vital issues in their music and their advocacy work. Songs like Mayfield's "People Get Ready" (1965) and Gaye's "What's Going On" (1971) were famous commentaries on social problems of the period.

Harry Belafonte speaks at a civil rights rally. *(Library of Congress)*

Today, many rappers are politically involved at all levels, from local grassroots efforts to international struggles. M1 (a.k.a. Mutulu Olugabala), a member of the activist rap duo Dead Prez, organized and became the local president of the Brooklyn Chapter of the National People's Democratic Uhuru Movement, an organization that defends the democratic rights of the African community. Beastie Boy Adam "MCA" Yauch took the lead in organizing the Tibetan Freedom Concert to raise awareness for Tibet's nonviolent struggle for independence from China, which has occupied its smaller neighbor since 1959. There have been four Tibetan Freedom Concerts since the first one took place in 1994.

Perhaps the best-known activist rapper is Chuck D, lyricist and lead vocalist for Public Enemy as well as a published author, radio show host, and spokesperson for the National Urban League, which worked with HSAN to establish the Hip-Hop Reader Program. Public Enemy is known for such controversial albums as *It Takes a Nation of Millions to Hold Us Back* (1988) and *Fear of a Black Planet* (1989), both released by Def Jam. Along with championing several political causes, Chuck D shares Simmons's opposition to legislative clampdowns on rap records with explicit content. Like many hip-hop activists, he considers rap music (which he has described as "the black CNN") a vital source of information about the real conditions that many poor Americans face.

One politician has shown that hip-hop is not just for the activists. Kwame Kilpatrick, who became the youngest mayor of any major U.S. city when he was elected Detroit's mayor in 2002, has been called America's hip-hop mayor. He has quoted Tupac Shakur in public statements and even used a rap track as his election campaign theme song. U.S. representative Maxine Waters of California has spoken about the value of the connection between young hip-hop fans and new leaders who have embraced the culture. "The rappers have helped to describe what's wrong in our society and the need to address it," she says. "That's a natural lead to politics and public policy. Now with people like [Kilpatrick] becoming part of the political process, it should all come together."

Apart from HSAN, Simmons has lobbied for other issues on which he has strong convictions, such as reforming New York State's Rockefeller drug laws and protesting cuts in public school funding. To change the Rockefeller laws, which call for mandatory sentences that many consider too severe, Simmons spoke with New York's governor, George Pataki, and the state's attorney general, Andrew Cuomo. He also lent his support to Hillary Rodham Clinton and Michael S. Steele in their campaigns for seats in the U.S. Senate.

In light of Simmons's new stances in the realm of politics, it was only logical that he would become a patron of an art form that encouraged political expression. The creative form that really impressed him was a performance art called slam poetry, or slam. As he had observed with the comedians of the chitlin circuit during the early 1990s, Simmons believed slam poets were underexposed.

The slam movement dated back decades; its evolution was influenced by the Last Poets, a collective of artists popular in the early 1970s, considered by some to be forerunners of rap music. Around the time Simmons was introduced to slam, poets were commonly performing in coffee shops and artist-friendly bars. In many places, poets competed against each other with the audience members acting as judges. During hip-hop's heyday in the 1990s, slam poetry began borrowing more from rap's vocal style.

It was Danny Simmons who brought slam poetry to his younger brother's attention. Danny had been asked by spoken-word poet Bruce George to help promote the underground movement. Danny knew that if there was anyone who could expose a fringe art form to a national audience, it was his brother. It took some convincing, but Simmons finally agreed to lend his name and the Def Jam logo to the project, and HBO agreed to air four episodes of *Russell Simmons Def Poetry* in 2001. Actor/rapper Mos Def was tapped to host the show and, as with *Def Comedy Jam*, Simmons appeared before the audience to close the program.

The reputable Def brand name helped make the first season of *Russell Simmons Def Poetry* a smash hit. With a diverse cast that included singer/songwriter Jewel, comedian Dave Chappelle, poet/playwright Amiri Baraka, and the Last Poets, the show drew many viewers who were not typically fans of poetry. Critics loved it too, and the show earned a Peabody Award, an honor recognizing excellence in radio

(From left) Mos Def, Alicia Keys, Simmons, and John Legend pose for a photo during a rehearsal for Russell Simmons's *Def Poetry Jam*. *(Courtesy of Scott Gries/Getty Images)*

and television. Once again, the mainstream had followed Simmons's lead in accepting a new cultural expression.

In 2002 Simmons's production team prepared to take Def Poetry beyond the television format. They realized that the dramatic force of the performances made it adaptable to the stage. Featuring the nine best poets from *Def Poetry*, a staged performance had a short run in San Francisco before it premiered in New York City as the *Def Poetry Jam on Broadway*. Reviewers appreciated the freshness of the material and the diversity of the cast. Because slam poetry was gaining popularity among high school and college students, the show's audience was also much younger than the typical crowd at a Broadway play. Along with being a commercial success, *Def Poetry Jam on Broadway* won a Tony Award for Special Theatrical Event.

While he poured himself into politics and fringe art forms, Simmons also continued to pay close attention to his commercial enterprises. His clothing company, now renamed Phat Fashions, continued to earn record profits, thanks largely to Kimora Lee Simmons's expansion of the Baby Phat line to include intimate apparel, accessories, footwear, fragrance, and jewelry. Like Simmons, she was able to use her own celebrity status to promote her apparel. (Kimora, who has been called the "First Lady of Hip Hop," could often be seen in public with a team of beauty assistants she called the "Glam Squad.") Baby Phat began doubling its size and by 2002, it reported $70 million in business, securing its place as the flagship division of Phat Fashions.

The success of Phat Fashions enabled the Simmonses to sell the company to Kellwood, a $2.2 billion clothing manufacturer, for $140 million in 2004. After the deal, both Simmons and Kimora stayed on as chief executives of their respective lines. Kimora continued to promote Baby Phat at nearly every opportunity, whether in magazine interviews or appearances on television programs like *America's Next Top Model* or the fashion-themed talk show *Life & Style*.

It is nearly inevitable that two businesspeople as ambitious as Russell and Kimora Simmons would butt heads sometimes. "We are fiercely competitive," Kimora admitted in an interview. Nonetheless, each spouse recognized the other's contributions toward Phat Fashions' triumph in the marketplace. She considers him her mentor, and he says she is the reason the company has done so well.

While building up Phat Fashions together, Simmons and Kimora also started a family. She gave birth to their first child, Ming Lee, in 2000, and had another daughter, Aoki Lee, in 2002. Simmons could not help gushing about his experiences as a new father. "[Ming Lee] grabs my arm and

Simmons and Kimora Lee pose with their children, Ming Lee (left) and Aoki. *(Courtesy of Johnny Nunez/WireImage)*

kisses it all of the time," he said. "I don't even know how to respond to it. It's the most beautiful thing. I would never have thought fatherhood was this great."

In 2001, the Simmons family moved into a new $14 million home in Saddle River, New Jersey. The 49,000-square-foot mansion is one of the largest homes on the East Coast. When the residence was featured on the lifestyle show *MTV Cribs*, viewers could take a tour through the Simmons's fifteen bedrooms, beauty salon, movie theater, and indoor and outdoor swimming pools. The stately rooms of the Simmons's mansion have also served as backdrops for Phat Fashions ads, many of which have featured Ming and Aoki wearing Baby Phat Girlz apparel.

At this stage in his life Simmons could have decided to retire from business and enjoy watching his children grow in their luxurious new home. But ultimately, he had something else in mind. While making millions may not have been important as it once was, he still considered business success "the vehicle that allows you to provide service." Furthermore, he remained invested in hip-hop and believed that some of its potential was still untapped. When he considered all the good things his celebrity and wealth had helped produce thus far, he wondered: what was possible if he became hip-hop's first billionaire?

EIGHT

Starting Over

In April 2005 Russell Simmons announced his newest venture, another record label called the Russell Simmons Music Group (RSMG). The label was a joint venture with, coincidentally, the Island Def Jam Music Group, which had been formed after Universal purchased Def Jam. Overseeing the deal was Shawn "Jay-Z" Carter, who had become president and CEO of Def Jam in 2005. In 1998 Simmons had helped negotiate the Def Jam deal to sign Carter and distribute releases from his independent label, Roc-a-Fella Records. Now, eight years later, two of hip-hop's biggest players had taken each other's places.

Simmons was not motivated by pride or money when he launched his new label. After succeeding in the game for more than two decades, he had nothing left to prove as an entrepreneur. But he still cared deeply about hip-hop, a passion he had made clear during 2004 in an open letter he wrote to *Billboard* magazine criticizing the leadership of Def Jam's president at the time, L. A. Reid. Few things were more rewarding for Simmons than collaborating with rappers. "I got back into the record business to get closer to the artist," he said at a press conference announcing the deal with Island Def Jam. "I want to do things that are inspiring."

Simmons was grateful to be working with the young

Shawn "Jay-Z" Carter *(Courtesy of AP Images/ Henny Ray Abrams)*

masterminds who now ran his former company. "The truth is as you get older you start looking to the younger people to inspire you, and Jay-Z has been a great inspiration," he said. For his part, Carter considered the deal with RSMG part of his education as a music industry CEO, saying, "We wanted to sign Russell so he could mentor me."

RSMG's first releases were by the German R&B girl group Black Buddafly and by Joey Simmons, who now went by the name Rev Run. (Run-D.M.C. had stopped performing after DJ Jam Master Jay was shot and killed in 2002.) Russell served as executive producer on Rev Run's 2005 solo album, *Distortion*, although the final product failed to live up to the past success of Run-D.M.C.'s heyday.

Rev Run (second from left) stands backstage with his family during an MTV show. *(Courtesy of AP Images/Jeff Christensen)*

The Simmons brothers have worked together in other areas as well. Joey Simmons is president of Phat Farm's line of sneakers and co-founded Run Athletics with his older brother. But the most successful collaboration between the two brothers was the television reality show *Run's House*, which became one of MTV's top-rated programs in 2005. Russell Simmons was executive producer of the show, which focused on the daily affairs of the rapper-turned-preacher, his wife, and their five children in their mansion in Saddle River, New Jersey, located just down the road from Simmons's own home. The show was a hit, and in 2007 it was renewed for a fourth season.

The success of *Run's House* begged the question: since Russell and Kimora are so comfortable in the limelight, why didn't they have their own reality show? It appears that even Simmons thinks there is a limit to how much exposure he can handle. "People don't need to see my underwear," he said.

While juggling his various entertainment ventures, Simmons continued to live out his philosophy of making profits so that he could provide the best service. He continually explored ways to fund HSAN's efforts. When he started a beverage company to sell DefCon3 in 2003, 100 percent of the product's sales went toward HSAN's activities. Simmons also designated 100 percent of sales of a fragrance, Phat Farm Atman, to various social causes. Similarly, a portion of sales of Phat Farm sneakers were reserved for HSAN. In an unusual marketing ploy, Simmons used a sales campaign for the sneakers as an opportunity to increase support for slave reparations, a political issue often addressed by HSAN and like-minded organizations. (The reparations movement has petitioned the U.S. government to provide financial compensation to the American descendants of slaves). Billboard advertisements for Phat Farm sneakers read, "Isn't it time for change? Economic justice now. Reparations now. It's an American justice issue."

There were other economic issues on Simmons's agenda. After he identified a lack of options for people with bad or nonexistent credit histories, his company UniRush Financial Services developed the Rush Card, a prepaid debit card that does not require its owner to open a bank account. The card proved to be an attractive product for some of the estimated 48 million Americans who do not have bank accounts. In the first eighteen months after the Rush Card's debut, 500,000 cards were reportedly distributed.

Simmons also recognized that many of these card buyers needed basic knowledge about how to bank and properly

Simmons speaks at a "Get Your Money Right" seminar. *(Courtesy of AP Images/Tom Gannam)*

build credit. In 2005 HSAN began holding a series of "Get Your Money Right" financial literacy seminars as part of the Financial Empowerment National Tour. Featuring author and personal finance expert Suze Orman, the tour continued into 2006, hitting many major U.S. and Canadian cities.

The appearances of high-profile rappers and R&B stars at the summits continued to draw attendees by the thousands. HSAN events in 2006 continued to bring out superstars like Snoop Dogg, Erykah Badu, Ludacris, and Young Jeezy. Simmons attributed the celebrities' passion to a new positive trend in the hip-hop community. "The collective consciousness of hip-hop is rising. There's no question about that," he said. It was yet another affirming development in the hip-hop industry that the CEO of rap had helped foster.

When Simmons foretold that hip-hop would be the new American mainstream, few believed its reach would be so extensive. In October 2003 the top ten songs on the *Billboard* chart all featured rap—a first in fifty years of the chart's history. The *Boston Globe* said the feat signaled "the culmination of hip-hop's ascent as the dominant force in popular music and culture."

As Simmons showed when he introduced Phat Farm in 1992, hip-hop is not just for music fans. Of the $10 billion that the hip-hop industry grosses annually, urban clothing accounts for $2 billion, or one-fifth of the market, according to the NPD Group, a market research company. Rocawear has surpassed Phat Fashions, reporting more than $700 million in annual retail sales, and in 2004 Sean John reaped annual U.S. sales of more than $450 million. Endorsements from big-name rappers like 50 Cent have sold as many sneakers as professional athletes do.

Now that hip-hop is recognized for its power to tell the truth about the street, as Simmons describes it, hip-hop music and culture has become a topic of academic study in the country's most prestigious institutions. More than thirty American universities include hip-hop in their study programs, including Harvard and the Massachusetts Institute of Technology (MIT). The Urban Think Tank Institute at Columbia University investigates and discusses issues and government policies that affect the hip-hop generation.

Part of the reason hip-hop has stayed relevant is that its unofficial spokesperson, Simmons, has maintained an interest in the industry that goes beyond seeking profits. The culture that Simmons and his peers have preserved still attracts artists with something meaningful to offer. Without hip-hop's greatest label, for example, there would not have been the same opportunities for Shawn "Jay-Z" Carter, a former drug dealer in Brooklyn's Marcy Projects who went on to sign with Def Jam and later became its president and CEO.

Simmons calls the successes of Jay-Z and a score of other rapper-CEOs "the best punk rock explosion of all time. In fact, it's ten times greater than anything punk rock ever achieved." Sean "Diddy" Combs, who is one of entertainment's most powerful figures, compliments Simmons for helping to maintain hip-hop's credibility and never compromising himself in the hundreds of business deals he has conducted: "He's taught us that you can go out there, get your money and be yourself, and you don't have to throw on your tap dancing shoes."

Even the world's foremost leaders have recognized hip-hop's cultural relevance. In 2006, the United Nations, the international organization that works toward improving economic development and the protection of human rights, recruited Simmons and HSAN to further its mission. In support of its Millennium Goals to fight global poverty, illness, and injustice, the United Nations asked Simmons, along with HSAN President Benjamin Chavis Muhammad, to be Goodwill Ambassadors, spokespeople for the rap community on some of the world's most vital issues. Simmons's assignment was to use hip-hop to raise awareness about war, poverty, HIV/ AIDS, and malnutrition. Simmons found the position to be very appropriate to HSAN's mission. "The underlying goal of the Hip-Hop Summit Action Network is to end poverty and ignorance," he said. "Our appointments to become United Nations Goodwill Ambassadors . . . will significantly enhance HSAN's global reach to further fulfill our mission."

Although Simmons and Kimora Lee filed for divorce in 2006, they remain close friends. *(Courtesy of AP Images/Richard Drew)*

However, despite his vast success, Simmons faced a major personal setback in 2006. In March, he announced that after eight years of marriage he and Kimora were filing for divorce. He moved out of the couple's New Jersey home and into a luxury apartment in New York City. Oddly enough, according to Simmons, their split did not have any impact on their business relationship at Phat Fashions. Furthermore, they still maintain a close friendship, spending long work-days together and even meeting for yoga sessions. Having such cordial relations has helped ensure their commitment to their children, who regularly see Simmons. They remain a great inspiration for him. "Hopefully I can do things that they're proud of," he says, "and that's a bigger agenda than I had before having these children."

Ever since booking his first show for Kurtis Blow, it seems that Simmons has been constantly expanding his agenda. His entrepreneurial genius enabled him to start a manage-ment company and independent record label on shoestring budgets and build them into a media empire. He convened a hip-hop summit that led to the creation of an internation-ally known political network and the registration of tens of thousands of young voters. World-famous individuals have come forward to help him with his grand projects, includ-ing fellow tycoons, multiplatinum rappers, Hollywood stars, scholars, and even international leaders.

But whatever the new program, political cause, or invest-ment venture, Russell Simmons will not let go of rap and its culture—a culture he has helped bring to the American mainstream and to the far corners of the globe. "Hip-hop has, in fact, changed the world. . . . And, I believe, we're far from through," he said. A bold claim, but at this point, who is going to dispute the Mogul of Rap?

Russell Simmons in 2006 *(Courtesy of AP Images)*

Timeline

1957   Born on October 4 in the Jamaica neighborhood of Queens, New York City.

1965   Simmons family moves to Hollis, Queens.

1975   Enrolls in City College of New York in Harlem.

1977   Promotes first major parties in Queens and Manhattan.

1979   With partners, produces and releases Kurtis Blow's "Christmas Rappin'," the first hip-hop record distributed by major label; establishes Rush Management, with Blow as first client.

1980   Books Kurtis Blow on national tour with the Commodores.

1981   Starts building up client roster with success of Blow's "Christmas Rappin'" and "The Breaks."

1982   Begins managing little brother, Joey (Run), and Darryl McDaniels (DMC), who make up two-thirds of the rap group Run-D.M.C.

1983   Coproduces Run-D.M.C.'s first single, "It's Like That"/"Sucker MCs"; negotiates the group's contract with Profile Records.

1984   Forms partnership with Rick Rubin; they launch Def Jam with release of LL Cool J's "I Need a Beat."

1985   Secures $2 million distribution deal for Def Jam with Columbia Records.

1986	Run-D.M.C.'s *Raising Hell*, coproduced by Simmons, becomes first hip-hop album to go platinum.
1988	Becomes sole head of Def Jam after Rubin leaves.
1990	Establishes, with partner Lyor Cohen, umbrella company Rush Associated Labels (RAL), which adds several imprint labels; finalizes negotiations on joint-venture deal with Sony Records.
1991	Begins producing HBO series *Russell Simmons's Def Comedy Jam*.
1992	Founds Phat Farm clothing line.
1993	Meets Kimora Lee at fashion show and begins dating her soon after.
1994	PolyGram buys Def Jam, relieving the label of its debt with Sony.
1995	Sells 50 percent of Def Jam Recordings to Polydor Records; co-founds Rush Philanthropic Arts Foundation with brothers Joey and Daniel.
1996	Founds Rush Media, an advertising company catering to the American youth culture market.
1998	Marries Kimora Lee, moves back to New York.
1999	Sells remaining stake in Def Jam for $130 million to Universal Music Group; establishes

partnership between Rush Advertising and the Deutsch Agency to form dRush.

2000 First child, Ming Lee, is born; launches Baby Phat line.

2001 Publishes autobiography, *Life and Def*; after organizing the first Hip Hop Summit, founds the Hip Hop Summit Action Network (HSAN); *Russell Simmons's Def Poetry* debuts on HBO.

2002 Daughter Aoki Lee is born; *Russell Simmons's Def Poetry Jam on Broadway* debuts.

2004 HSAN reveals the Hip Hop Reader Program and holds several summits that register thousands of new voters; sells Phat Fashions for $140 million.

2005 Establishes the Russell Simmons Music Group (RSMG), a joint-venture label with Island Def Jam Music Group; produces *Run's House*, a reality show starring Rev Run (Joey Simmons).

2006 Receives appointment as UN Goodwill Ambassador to raise awareness for war, poverty and HIV/AIDS; announces that he is filing for divorce with Kimora Lee.

Source Notes

CHAPTER ONE: Street Smart

p. 11, "When we moved . . ." Russell Simmons, *Life and Def: Sex, Drugs, Money, and God* (New York: Three Rivers Press, 2001), 15.

p. 12, "even by criminals," Stacy Gueraseva, *Def Jam, Inc.* (New York: OneWorld, 2005), 22.

p. 12, "Perhaps I've been good . . ." Simmons, *Life and Def*, 14.

p. 14, "To me the coolest stuff . . ." Ibid., 24.

p. 14, "very ghetto and gritty," Ibid., 26.

p. 15, "the force in college parties," Ibid., 40.

p. 18, "spirit of openhearted innocence," Nelson George, *Hip Hop America* (New York: Penguin Books, 1998), 20.

CHAPTER TWO: Reproducing the Street Sound

p. 21, "didn't truly reflect . . . " Simmons, *Life and Def*, 53.

p. 22, "I ran downstairs . . ." Ibid., 54.

p. 22, "I got on a plane . . ." Russell Simmons, "The Honorees: Russell Simmons (interview)," VH-1 Hip-Hop Honors, http://www.vh1.com/shows/events/hip_hop_honors/2006/honoree_detail.jhtml?honoree=russellsimmons.

p. 25, "the single most creative thing . . . " Simmons, *Life and Def*, 65.

p. 27, "I can't believe you made . . ." Gueraseva, *Def Jam, Inc.*, 33.

p. 27, "hit records in the making," Alex Ogg, *The Men Behind Def Jam* (London: Omnibus Press, 2002), 25–26.

p. 28, "like a substitute teacher," Gueraseva, *Def Jam, Inc.*, 34.

p. 29, "It's a hit, it's fantastic!" Ibid., 40.

p. 29, "Let's do this together. . . ." Ibid.

p. 30, "mogul of rap," Simmons, *Life and Def*, 99.

CHAPTER THREE: Rockin' the Suburbs

p. 32, "The fact is . . ." Simmons, *Life and Def*, 100.

p. 34, "Basically I urged them . . ." Ibid., 92.

p. 35, "was one of the . . ." George, *Hip Hop America*, 66.

p. 37, "The company always was . . ." Gueraseva, *Def Jam, Inc.*, 92.

p. 37, "creative, supportive, and mad open," Simmons, *Life and Def*, 84.

p. 40, "a real cultural . . . " Ibid., 108.

p. 40, "Rap will be a fixture . . ." Stephen Holden, "A Young Company Guides Rap Music into the Mainstream," *New York Times*, August 11, 1987, C13.

p. 41, "To be single, black, and . . ." Simmons, *Life and Def*, 104.

p. 42, "I hate this . . ." Gueraseva, *Def Jam, Inc.*, 163.

p. 43, "I was a manager . . ." Christopher Vaughn, "Russell Simmons's Rush for Profits," *Black Enterprise*, December 1992, 72.

p. 45, "charm school," Arthur Kempton, "The Lost Tycoons: The Fall of the Black Empires," *New York Review of Books*, June 10, 1999, 51.

p. 45, "I see hip-hop culture . . ." Simmons, *Life and Def*, 4.

p. 45, "reaching blacks or whites . . ." Ibid., 80.

CHAPTER FOUR: Creating a Hip-Hop Brand

p. 47-48, "Def Jam does not . . ." Gueraseva, *Def Jam, Inc.*, 164.

p. 48, "I was feeling mad pressure," Simmons, *Life and Def*, 112.

p. 49, "Def Jam brand seem larger . . ." Ibid., 113.

p. 51, "That jet-setting crowd carries messages . . ." Ibid., 165.

p. 53, "more upscale and aspirational," Ibid., 155.

p. 54, "the underground economy of black culture," Devin Friedman, "Notes from the New Chitlin Circuit," *GQ*, June 1999, 241.

p. 55, "*Def Comedy Jam* degenerated . . ." Ibid., 271.

p. 55, "Segregated comedy is sad . . ." Ibid., 272.

CHAPTER FIVE: Feeling the Heat

p. 54, "Good night. God bless," Simmons, *Life and Def*, 223.

p. 57, "There was a lot . . ." Ibid., 127.

p. 58, "really felt like the label . . ." Gueraseva, *Def Jam, Inc.*, 196.

p. 58, "withdrawn a little bit . . ." Ibid., 208.

p. 59, "I'm not running . . ." Kevin Chappell, "The Half-Billion-Dollar Hip-Hop Empire of Russell Simmons," *Ebony*, July 2003, 174.

p. 63, "When you wanna close . . ." Gueraseva, *Def Jam, Inc.*, Ibid., 261.

p. 65, "[N]o one called . . ." Simmons, *Life and Def*, 185.

p. 65, "I was 38 . . ." Ibid., 187.

p. 65, "What [politicians] should be focusing . . ." Ibid., 190.

CHAPTER SIX: A Quieted Mind

p. 68, "I got addicted right away," Cathleen Falsani, *The God Factor* (New York: Sarah Crichton Books, 2005), 220.

p. 69, "Yoga changed my life dramatically . . ." Chappell, "The Half-Billion-Dollar Hip-Hop Empire of Russell Simmons," 178.

p. 72, "the truth is . . ." Simmons, *Life and Def*, 195.

p. 72, "The Greatest MCs of All Time," mtv.com, 2006, http://www.mtv.com/bands/h/hip_hop_week/2006/emcees.

p. 73, "the face of the 21st century," Nancy Jo Sales, "Unbearable Fabulosity," *Vanity Fair*, April 2005, 244.

p. 73, "Russell Effect," Dr. Richard Oliver and Tim Leffel, *Hip-Hop, Inc.* (New York: Thunder's Mouth Press, 2006), 79.

CHAPTER SEVEN: Assembling an Army

p. 74, "[T]he only real happiness . . ." Simmons, *Life and Def*, 219.

p. 75, "The hip hop community moves . . ." Ogg, *The Men Behind Def Jam*, 217–18.

p. 77, "the artistic presentation . . ." Russell Simmons, "Hip-Hop Fridays: Statements of Senator Joseph Lieberman And Russell Simmons On Entertainment Ratings Systems," Blackelectorate.com, July 25, 2001, http://www.black electorate.com/articles.asp?ID=384.

p. 77-78, "The Hip-Hop Summit Action Network . . ." Quoted in Russell Simmons and Benjamin Muhammad, "Power Movement: The National Agenda of the Hip-Hop Summit Action Network," *The Source*, June 2002, 73.

p. 78, "How you gonna be . . ." Ta-Nehisi Coates, "Compa$$ionate Capitali$m," *Village Voice*, January 7–13, 2004, 32.

p. 79, "When [P. Diddy] says register . . ." Ibid., 28.

p. 80, "hip-hop activism," Jeff Chang, *Can't Stop Won't Stop* (New York: St. Martin's 2005), 249.

p. 82, "the black CNN," Quoted in L. Christopher Smith, "The Big Sellout," *Rolling Stone*, December 15, 2005, 114.

p. 82, "The rappers have helped . . ." Geoff Boucher, "Hip-Hop Is 'Music That Speaks' to Young Voters," *Los Angeles Times*, May 11, 2003, A22.

p. 85, "First Lady of Hip Hop. . ." Sales, "Unbearable Fabulosity," 242, 274.

p. 85, "We are fiercely competitive," Charlie Rose, "Russell Simmons, Unplugged," *60 Minutes II*, February 11, 2004, http://www.cbsnews.com/stories/2004/02/09/60II/main598970.shtm.

p. 85-86, "[Ming Lee] grabs my arm . . . ." Chappell, "The Half-Billion-Dollar Hip-Hop Empire of Russell Simmons," 178.

p. 87, "the vehicle that allows you . . ." David Liss, "Ask the CEO," *Business Week Online*, January 13, 2004, http://www.businessweek.com/bwdaily/dnflash/jan2004/nf20040113_4406_db074.htm.

CHAPTER EIGHT: Starting Over

p. 89, "I got back into the . . ." Tracey Ford, "Hip-hop impresario forms new partnership with Def Jam," *Rolling Stone*, April 13, 2005, http://www.rollingstone.com/news/story/7249573/simmons_launches_label.

p. 89, "The truth is . . ." Ibid.

p. 91, "We wanted to sign Russell . . ." Ibid.

p. 91, "People don't need to see . . ." Russell Simmons and Julie Schlosser, "Russell Simmons Wants You—To Vote," *Fortune*, May 17, 2004, 41.

p. 92, "Isn't it time for change? . . ." Coates, "Compa$$ionate Capitali$m," 28.

p. 93, "The collective consciousness of hip-hop . . ." Simmons and Schlosser, "Russell Simmons Wants You—To Vote," 41.

p. 94, "the culmination of hip-hop's ascent . . ." Joan Anderman, "Hip-hop setting the beat," *Boston Globe*, October 4 2003.

p. 94, "the best punk rock explosion . . ." Simmons, *Life and Def*, 209.

p. 94, "He's taught us that you . . ." Ogg, *The Men Behind Def Jam*, 149.

p. 94, "The underlying goal of the . . ." Russell Simmons, "Russell Simmons to Be Named U.N. Goodwill Ambassador," Mediabistro.com, July 24, 2006, http://www.mediabistro.com/fishbowlny/pop_culture/ russell_simmons_to_be_named_un_goodwill_ ambassador_40700.asp.

p. 96, "Hopefully I can do things . . ." Simmons, "The Honorees: Russell Simmons (interview)," VH-1 Hip-Hop Honors, http://www.vh1.com/shows/events/ hip_hop_honors/2006/honoree_detail.jhtml?honoree= russellsimmons.

p. 96, "Hip-hop has . . ." Simmons, *Life and Def*, 9.

Bibliography

Anderman, Joan. "Hip-hop setting the beat." *Boston Globe*, October 4, 2003.

Berfield, Susan. "The CEO of Hip Hop." *Business Week*, October 17, 2003.

Boucher, Geoff. "Hip-Hop Is 'Music That Speaks' to Young Voters." *Los Angeles Times*, May 11, 2003, A22.

Brackey, Harriet Johnson. "Music Mogul Pushes Pre-paid Visa Cards." Knight-Ridder Tribune Business News, July 14, 2005.

Chang, Jeff. *Can't Stop Won't Stop*. New York: St. Martin's, 2005.

Chappell, Kevin. "The CEO of Hip-hop." *Ebony*, January 2001.

———. "The Half-Billion-Dollar Hip-Hop Empire of Russell Simmons." *Ebony*, July 2003.

Coates, Ta-Nehisi. "Compa$$ionate Capitali$m." *Village Voice*, January 7–13, 2004.

Curan, Catherine. "Def-ening the Nation." *Crain's New York Business*, April 28, 2003.

Falsani, Cathleen. *The God Factor:* New York: Sarah Crichton Books, 2005.

Ford, Tracey. "Simmons Launches Label." *Rollingstone. com*, April 13, 2005. http://www.rollingstone.com/news/

story/7249573/simmons_launches_label (accessed
September 2007).

Friedman, Devin. "Notes from the New Chitlin Circuit."
Gentleman's Quarterly, June 1999.

George, Nelson. *Hip Hop America*. New York: Penguin Books,
1998.

Gueraseva, Stacy. *Def Jam, Inc.* One World: New York,
2005.

Holden, Stephen. "A Young Company Guides Rap Music
into the Mainstream." *New York Times*, August 11, 1987.

Hughes, Alan. "Phat Profits." *Black Enterprise*, June 2002.

Kempton, Arthur. "The Lost Tycoons: The Fall of the
Black Empires." *New York Review of Books*, June
10, 1999.

Liss, David. "Ask the CEO." *Business Week Online*, January
13, 2004. http://www.businessweek.com/bwdaily/dnflash/
jan2004/nf20040113_4406_db074.htm. (accessed
September 2007).

Norfleet, Dawn M. "Hip-Hop and Rap." *African American
Music: An Introduction*. Oxford, England: Taylor &
Francis, 2004.

Ogg, Alex. *The Men Behind Def Jam*. London: Omnibus
Press, 2002.

Oliver, Dr. Richard, and Tim Leffel. *Hip-Hop, Inc.* New
York: Thunder's Mouth Press, 2006.

Posner, Gerald. *Motown*. New York: Random House, 2002.

Roberts, Johnnie L. "Beyond Definition." *Newsweek*, July
28, 2003.

"Russell Simmons to Be Named U.N. Goodwill Ambassador."
Mediabistro.com, July 24, 2006. http://www.mediabistro.
com/fishbowlny/pop_culture/russell_simmons_to_be_
named_un_goodwill_ambassador_40700.asp (accessed
September 2007).

Rose, Charlie. "Russell Simmons, Unplugged." *60 Minutes II*, February 11, 2004. http://www.cbsnews.com/stories/2004/02/09/60II/main598970.shtml.

Sales, Nancy Jo. "Unbearable Fabulosity." *Vanity Fair*, April 2005.

Simmons, Russell. *Life and Def.* In collaboration with Nelson George. New York: Three Rivers Press, 2001.

———. "Hip-Hop Fridays: Statements of Senator Joseph Lieberman and Russell Simmons on Entertainment Ratings Systems." Blackelectorate.com, http://www.blackelectorate.com/articles.asp?ID=384 (accessed September 2007).

"The Honorees: Russell Simmons (interview)," *VH-1 Hip-Hop Honors 2006*, January 12, 2006. http://www.vh1.com/shows/events/hip_hop_honors/2006/honoree_detail.jhtml?honoree=russellsimmons (accessed September 2007).

———. "Respecting the Living Legacy of Def Jam: An Open Letter to the Recording Industry from Russell Simmons." *Billboard*, August 21, 2004.

———. "Russell Simmons Interview." *Fresh Air from WHYY.* November 27, 2001. http://www.npr.org/templates/story/story.php?storyId=4823677 (accessed September 2007).

Simmons, Russell, and Julie Schlosser. "Russell Simmons Wants You—To Vote." *Fortune*, May 17, 2004.

Simmons, Russell, and Benjamin Muhammad. "Power Movement: The National Agenda of the Hip-Hop Summit Action Network." *The Source*, June 2002.

Smith, L. Christopher. "The Big Sellout." *Rolling Stone*, December 15, 2005.

Vaughn, Christopher. "Russell Simmons's Rush for Profits." *Black Enterprise*, December 1992.

Web sites

http://www.hsan.org
The official Web site of the Hip-Hop Summit Action Network, a political action committee formed in 2001.

http://www.defjam.com
Web site of the music label co-founded by Russell Simmons.

http://www.rushphilanthropic.org
The nonprofit organization's Web site includes its latest news, mission statement, and a review of its programs.

http://www.vh1.com/artists/az/simmons_russell/bio.jhtml
This page features an overview of Simmons's career and has hyperlinks to the many people who have crossed the mogul's path during his long career.

http://www.lemonadestories.com/defjam.html
This firsthand account by Simmons is drawn from *Lemonade Stories*, a documentary about successful entrepreneurs.

http://www.rollingstone.com
The online version of *Rolling Stone* magazine is a good resource for reading more about Simmons and the artists he has worked with over the years.

Index